GOD WILL WORK <u>WITH</u> YOU

BUT NOT <u>FOR</u> YOU

Lao Russell

Sincerely, Lao Russell

GOD WILL WORK <u>WITH</u> YOU

BUT NOT <u>FOR</u> YOU

A LIVING PHILOSOPHY

BY

Lao Russell

UNIVERSITY OF SCIENCE AND PHILOSOPHY

FORMERLY THE WALTER RUSSELL FOUNDATION

SWANNANOA, WAYNESBORO, VIRGINIA 22980

First   Edition 1955   10,000
Second Edition 1956   10,000
Third Edition 1969   10,000

To God, and the Unity of
His One-World-Family,
this book is humbly dedicated.

God's Great Gifts to Man Are Life and That Which Man Calls Death.

God's universe is based upon the Love which He gives to His universal body as Life—and the Love that His universal body regives to Him as Death for eternal re-borning as Life.

THIS NEW WAY OF LIFE

is based upon the balanced perfection and normalcy of the Love Principle of Nature which never takes, but gives for the purpose of equally regiving that which has been given.

LIFE

is the great gift of Love which our Father-Mother has given to all Creation—and

DEATH

is the great gift of Love which all Creation regives to our Father-Mother for eternally resurrecting all Creation into equally balanced and divided two-way life sequences for ever and ever.

Lao Russell

Basic Foundation for a
Living Philosophy

To bring blessings upon yourself bless your neighbor.

To enrich yourself enrich your neighbor.

Honor your neighbor and the world will honor you.

To sorely hurt yourself hurt your neighbor.

He who seeks love will find it by giving it.

The measure of a man's wealth is the measure of wealth he has given.

To enrich yourself with many friends enrich your friends with yourself.

That which you take away from any man the world will take away from you.

When you take the first step to give yourself to that which you want, it will also take its first step to give itself to you.

Peace and happiness do not come to you from your horizon, they spread from you out to infinity beyond your horizon.

The whole universe is a mirror which reflects back to you that which you reflect forward into it.

Love is like unto the ascent of a mountain. It comes ever nearer to you as you go ever nearer to it.

Lao Russell

OTHER BOOKS BY LAO RUSSELL

LOVE—A Scientific and Living Philosophy of
Love and Sex

An Eternal Message of Light and Love

LAO RUSSELL, *Co-Author, with* WALTER RUSSELL,

Scientific Answer to Human Relations

Atomic Suicide?

The World Crisis—Its Explanation and Solution

The One-World Purpose—A Plan to Dissolve War
by a Power More Mighty Than War

and

One Year Home Study Course

of

Universal Law, Natural Science
and Living Philosophy

Introduction

by

Walter Russell

To introduce one's own wife to the world naturally leads to the temptation of exaggeration. I feel myself immunized from that, however, by the impossibility of it. I feel that I can say, without prejudice, and quite free from the fact of her relation to me, that hers is the greatest mentality I have ever known. That is saying much for me for it has been my privilege to intimately know the greatest intellectuals of our time.

My wife was born with the spirit of the Crusader in her very first life's breath. It was her destiny to search from early childhood for the illusive secret which alone would free man from his belief in EVIL, which seemingly enslaved him.

She, likewise, journeyed in far lands in her search for that secret which would awaken the Light in man and thus release him from the chains of his dark. 'Neath the pyramids of Sahara's sands, to tropics of the Indies, and in crowded cities of four continents, she searched—but she did not look outside of man for that which she sought. She looked only within him. She looked only into the Light of his illumined Soul. And it was there in his illumined Soul she found the Holy Grail of her long search. For behold! all that she found there was GOOD—naught but GOOD.

And again she journeyed far throughout the world to look into the Soul of Man to find that which he calls EVIL—but always and forever she found naught but GOOD in the SOUL of Man.

Wondering much where EVIL could be found in him she looked again into his SENSES, and behold! she found EVIL there, close wrapped in a black shroud of fear and greed that led men to deep chasms filled with phantom gold, which man could never even hold to count—so quickly did it disappear into its black shroud. Looking again more closely to find why the senses of man led him to do these many things, which he called evil, she saw within that black shroud a phantom named BELIEF IN EVIL, which his senses made into his own image to become that which he believes himself to be.

While looking into the hearts of men and women who were fathers and mothers of a disunited unhappy, fearing world, she was compelled to seek the cause of that disunity and dissolve world-fear and unhappiness. Her Cosmic Illumining lead her to envision the cause of world-disunity and mankind's lack of knowledge of the meaning of Love. "Man is not bad," she said: "He is not evil. There is no sin anywhere. There is naught but GOOD. Man is still in his early dawn and does not yet know how to live, or how to love. He does not yet know WHO he is, or WHY he is here. Too few among men have yet awakened to their divinity. Therefore, while man is still so new he must be forgiven, for as Jesus said: 'They know not what they do.'"

Being God-taught through her Soul, rather than through her senses, she knew the realities which the senses can never reach. Likewise, she was freed from the illusions of matter in motion which so greatly deceive the senses that look upon transciency as real. That is why she looked out upon God's universe with eyes of inner vision to know the unseen, and with inner ears to hear that which is still enfolded within the silences. That is why she has always sought within her Self for that which she wished to know and for guidance toward that destiny which was commanded of her to fulfill.

This marvelous message which she has been prepared to give to the world through much communion with God, her only teacher, is the consummation of the task God set for her. She hereby gives God's message to the world to void its dangerous tensions and reverse its downward plunge toward the oblivion for which it is unknowingly heading.

My beloved wife is a messenger who bears new knowledge to mankind, much needed by him in this dire hour of twilight, which will either illumine him in a new dawn or engulf him in another long night. God has sent many messages of love to man, by many messengers, to uplift him to high pinnacles from which man has always fallen, and will continue to fall until he listens with inner ears to these messages from Soul of God to Soul of man.

God's Silent Voice forever speaks to all men, but few hear it, and the vast many know not what it means. The very few who do hear it, and know its meaning, bring messages of Love to those who do not know its meaning to tell them what Love means.

Man has never known the meaning of these Cosmic Messages of Love, for man the father of the world-family is not of himself alone. It has been but a scant generation since he resistingly allowed the mother of the world-family to come to the very edge of his portals in just one little corner of the world.

All her life, my wife has known that the cause of all world-disaster and disunity has been because the world-family is without a mother. That which happens to one motherless home is happening to the whole world-home. God made fathers and mothers to share equally in the building of their homes. Where man is master in his home love and unity cannot abide therein. Until man knows God's law and shares equally with women in the management of the great world-home, there will be the disunity of a warring world of fear unto the end of eternity. Civilization will forever fall as this one is now falling until the one-whole-world-family is equally balanced by the qualities of both the father and the mother.

Since her early childhood my illumined Lao has held to that vision of the great world-fault, and to the conviction that her destiny compelled her to arouse all thinking men and women to the necessity of uniting as One Father-Mother to bring love, romance, peace and happiness to this unhappy fearing world.

The message contained herein is the first step toward that world-transformation. The next step must be initiated by women who will be aided by the most liberal of intellectual men to bring a *balanced civilization* into being, which will endure forever.

Table of Contents

PART I

"I must say to myself that I ruined myself,
and that nobody great or small
can be ruined save by his own hand."

OSCAR WILDE.

CHAPTER I

The Eleventh Hour

This message is given to man in the Eleventh Hour of his threatened fall into another terrifying abyss of oblivion. It is written from the depths of my Soul with the earnest desire that it will not be a lost voice crying in the wilderness.

Once more man's hard-built civilization has all the evidence of another fall into the chaos and oblivion of another dark age, and for the same reason it has always fallen. Up to the year 1900 the world had steadily progressed for eight centuries, but since that time it has fallen to lower levels than it had risen in those eight long centuries of upward struggle.

The world was very friendly about the turn of the century. Wars, and the threat of wars, seemed to have passed out of world-thinking. The pent up hates of empire building days were seemingly forgotten. World armament for the protection of neighbor against neighbor had practically ceased. Warships seemed useless and were destroyed by many great nations. Culture was at a high level all over the world. Day by day great art salons and musical events multiplied and geniuses were patronized to make the cultural world more beautiful.

Then suddenly, in 1914, the old traits of the jungle reappeared and man once more became the killer and slaughterer. Only this time he killed and slaughtered on

3

the greatest scale ever known. Increasing world-unity disappeared and an unprecedented world-disunity intensified. Hatred, fear, enmity, cruelty and debauchery returned from its forgotten grave and shed the blood of over forty million human beings in thirty years, besides enslaving countless millions of once free men. Cruelty unknown to the world, even in its two inquisitions, became commonplace.

Never before in human history had nations enslaved their own people. They made slaves of conquered tribes or of other races, but never their own people, as part of this world has done and is still doing. Millions of our brothers, whom we should love, we steamed and baked alive in huge furnaces. Whole regiments were buried alive in graves they were forced to dig for their own burial. Brain washing added a new and undreamed of cruelty to man's category of heinous crimes.

Today the whole world is divided against itself and must fall unless love and service come quickly enough to save it. No house can be divided against itself and survive —whether it be one home or a world of homes. If multiplied scientific power causes another Armageddon in our divided world, the civilization we have known will end.

It is as impossible for peace to come by waging war as it is impossible for love to come by hating. Man wages war in the hope of finding peace, never realizing that the only fruit of war is war and any seeming peace is but a truce of fear between wars. Have we not suffered enough to say: Lord save us from ourselves, lest we destroy ourselves? Or must we suffer more and still more until there are too few left to fight?

God's plan is for man to learn the lesson of Love, upon which the universe is based. He can learn that lesson only

by giving love to his neighbor, for regiving by his neighbor. Service to one's neighbor is the highest principle of
life. The value of every man to every other man is the
greatest source of man's wealth and prosperity. World
peace and happiness can only be acquired by the realization of man's asset value to man, and the conservation of
that value by mutual service.

Instead of that practice mankind has been engaged in
the lowest conceivable practice, which is man-killing for
greed. Over sixty million men have been employed for
forty years in making man-killing the greatest of all world
industries. Over four hundred billion dollars have been
spent to kill men instead of obeying the brotherhood-of-
man law. Man-killing itself was insignificant in numbers
during past centuries. Its growth has been so rapid that
our modern civilization has killed thirty times as many
humans in fifty years as the total number killed in the
five centuries preceding the seventeenth century.

The difficulty in killing men was great when the bow
and arrow was the principle weapon. It became increasingly easy to kill men as the bullet, projectile, torpedo,
undersea boat and bomber plane supplanted the bow and
arrow. It is now possible to kill every man, woman and
child within a radius of twenty miles with only one bomb.
Surely the ease of killing men has multiplied to undreamed of proportions when we can now kill five times
as many men in a few minutes as Napoleon killed in all
of his campaigns!

Is it not time, therefore, that thinking men should get
together and look at our degenerating selves as we really
are, instead of through a rosy mirror which pictures our
brutal, barbarian, cruel civilization with an unearned
halo of glory? Have we sufficient strength of character to

admit that every high stage of our prosperity has been acquired by plunder, piracy, slave making, slave dealing, and vast exploitation of the weak, by the might-of-greed in man?

Is it not also time to give deep thought to the fact that our strictly *man-ruled* world has always been a warring world? Man has always expressed man-nature, inherited from his primate fighting jungle days, by marauding, conquering, piracy, slavery and killing for greed, while women have loved, and served, and given life to the world. Where man and woman work together as one, to make a happy home, they always succeed. Might it not be that a happy world is as impossible without the romance of unity and equality of world fathers and mothers, as a happy home would be? Man-greed of man the conqueror and warrior has made the kind of world which faces us today. With love and romance crucified by greed what hope is there for survival?

There is only one sure way to save mankind from his threatened self-annihilation, and that one way is through new knowledge of man himself—dynamic knowledge of: Who he is; What he is; Why he is here; What his relationship to other men is; What his relationship to God and His universe is. With this basic knowledge he will know his purpose on earth, and knowingly work *with* God who created him, instead of destroying himself by his own hand in working against God, as he is now doing.

Ever since man emerged from the jungle of his beginnings he has been trying to discover himself. Ever since that Silent Voice within him began to be faintly heard at the dawn of his Consciousness, he has been forever asking: WHO am I? WHAT am I? WHY am I here?

Long centuries have passed and man still asks those

unanswered questions. Man himself is the greatest mystery of the as yet unknown. He has conquered the seas, the skies, the elements and the very forces which move the universe. Man, the great discoverer of many things, has not yet discovered himself. He does not yet know MAN. He still despairingly asks: WHO am I? WHAT am I? WHY am I here?

The time has come when man can know if he will but listen with inner ears to the Silent Voice within himself. There have been those in past ages who have made that supreme discovery. These have tried to tell others, but their words had no meaning for primate man.

Then came the supreme One who knew. He tried to tell man of his divine heritage, and of his God of Love, and of his Oneness with Him and with all men, but He died on the Cross. His words had no meaning for primate man of that day. They still continued to worship a God of Fear, a wrathful God whom they sought to appease with blood sacrifice.

Even unto this day, mankind has never fully comprehended the teachings of Jesus, the consummate scientist of all time, whose few words contain the greatest knowledge ever given to man. In them is the complete answer to the identity and *purpose* of man. In them is also all knowledge of Cause, for which world renowned scientists have so hopelessly sought. These still ask: Who am I? What is gravity—and energy—and light—and what holds the atom together? Jesus plainly answered even these questions for the future ages of man and pointed the way to their understanding, but men looked, and still continue to look, the other way. They do not comprehend.

Even though men crucified Jesus, the divine Messenger of Love, who brought GOOD into the world to supplant

evil, there were those who believed on Him. Love sur-
vived its crucifixion, even though those few who believed
on Him, with great faith, did not comprehend His deeper
meanings. There are but few in our world of today who
comprehend His deeper meanings.

*God, man, woman, and Nature are the only elements
man has to know, and to interrelate, in order to build an
enduring civilization.* Man's lack of knowledge of these
elements, and how to interrelate them, has caused his
hard-built civilizations to fall many times, as it is again
about to fall unless man can "be transformed by the renewing of his Mind" in time to save himself from that
dread catastrophe.

This new concept is, in reality, a new understanding
and a new interpretation of the teachings of Jesus, the
only fully-illumined Christ Conscious mystic of all time.
Jesus gave to the world a complete way of life which
would have endured forever if men had but comprehended Him. Man was still too new, too close to the jungle of his primate days, to even faintly comprehend Him.

People of this electric, radio-conscious age are now fully
able to comprehend His teachings if they will but throw
off old pagan traditions which have been too securely riv-
eted into the thinking of this age. If Jesus were here today
to give to the world His supreme knowledge, *His greatest
obstacle would be in overcoming the pagan misinterpre-
tations of His own teachings, which have built an impreg-
nable wall of superstition, evil, magic and belief in the
miraculous and supernatural, around man's thinking.*
When one realizes that many of our highest intellectuals
believed in witchcraft and burned witches alive within
the last two hundred years, it is easy to see how strong a
hold early pagan thinking has upon modern thinking.

This will be the greatest obstacle in presenting the real meaning of Jesus' teachings herein. There are many, however, who are ready for new comprehension. If those who read these teachings are sufficiently open-minded to accept them, then we can in fact save this world from its threatened oblivion and replace it with an enduring world of peace, happiness and good will to men. This high pinnacle can be reached only by unifying the whole world into one family.

Let us, therefore, transform the world by the renewing of the world-Mind. *That transformation can take place only by acquiring knowledge of man's inseparable and eternal moment to moment unity with a comprehensible God, and of man's unity with man, woman, and Nature.*

The world could have had a dynamic knowledge of God, and of His relationship with man, long ago, instead of the vague imaginings it now has, if it had comprehended Jesus' teachings. He told man to look *within* himself to find the answer to all things.

What did He mean by that? What is there *within* man which could be "the kingdom of heaven," and all things else?

He meant MIND. *He meant that all there is in this universe is Mind and body—which means Creator and Creation, and which also means Cause and Effect.*

And that IS the answer to all things. It is the complete answer to what God, Nature, man-woman, energy, silence, sound, stillness, motion, and all things else, are.

God's Mind, and the electric pulsations of His divided thinking, constitute the entirety of this universe. Beyond that there is naught else.

God's omniscient, omnipotent, living, conscious Mind is eternally at rest.

God's electric thinking is eternally in motion. His electric, creative thinking extends from centers of stillness to create bodies, which live for a period of time, to manifest His knowledge of power and action. All living bodies thus extended from Him to express His energy by action, must then return to Him for a period of rest, before again extending into another pulsation of action. This is the principle known as reincarnation or repetition of body patterns, which is the characteristic process of Nature.

Man conceives these thought-pulsations of the living, thinking God, to be living and dying bodies of people, who have identity and reality. In this tragic misconception lies all the ills which man has made for himself, all of them, without exception, from business failures to divorces, from degenerative diseases to wars, from frustrations to insanity, and from the periodic rise and fall of whole civilizations.

Oh, the pity of it! And WHY?

Simply because men of that day did not comprehend what Jesus meant when He plainly told them that *they could find God within themselves and then all things else would be added unto them.* Instead of comprehending and believing Him, the mass-Mind of the world, then and now, looks outward toward transient, pulsing bodies of living-dying physical matter for their realities, instead of to their centering, spiritual Soul-Mind. Man did just the opposite of what Jesus taught, and made for himself a way of life which has always led to catastrophe and oblivion.

He looked outside of himself for his sense of values and chose transient, pulsing, living-dying bodies of material things for his choice possessions, which he thought would enrich him.

He looked away from his spiritual Self to find love and happiness in mere sensation of interchange with physical bodies of pulsing motion, which had naught but motion in them to give.

He looked away from the One great reality within which all power reposed, into the unreality of transient materialism for the power he coveted, and took unto himself a mirage which dissolved itself in its own emptiness.

Even the greatest of intellectuals looked the other way, away from the still fulcrum source of all energy, to endow pulsing vibrations of motion with energy. Even they looked for CAUSE in the transient EFFECTS of cause.

Is it any wonder then that the old way of life which man has chosen to follow has never led him to happiness and peace? Has any way of life ever led to happiness, peace and prosperity, which was based upon greed for material possessions and power?

Not one thing of man's creating has endured when man looked outward, and away from the spirit which centered him.

On the other hand, those immortal creations of man which have endured, and will endure as long as civilization lasts, are those works of the spiritual geniuses who have been illumined by the awakening of that divine spark which centers every man. Such words are created in the ecstasy and inspiration of their Mind-Source and reflect the rhythms of God's thinking in them, while the works of man-bodies, who know naught but the rhythms of body sounds, live but for the day and are forgotten.

The new way of life, which is based upon God-awareness within, is now necessary, else we perish. Man's old way of life has always built a world of fear, hatred, enmity and disunity, the policy being to take from his neighbor that which he wanted for himself by the power of might over right.

The old way which has proved so disastrous was based upon *taking*—which created enemies who show their hatred by *retaking*.

The new way will be based upon *giving*—which creates friends who show their love by *regiving*.

In my husband's "Message of the Divine Iliad" are these words: "All men shall come to Me in due time, but theirs is the agony of awaiting."

By working knowingly with God's universal laws, our present "agony of awaiting" can be over, and all men and women can look forward to living in heavenly peace and happiness as one united world-family. It is a tremendous challenge and a tremendous goal, but it is a prize in which all mankind can share.

CHAPTER II

Who Am I?

Who am I? What am I? Why am I here? Man has eternally sought for the answers to these vital questions all down the long ages.

The great fact of life is that life must be lived and man's strongest instinct is to live. He tenaciously clings to life with all the zeal of his being. He does not yet know who he is—his identity—his individuality—what he is, or the WHY of so many things which bewilder him. Day by day he faces that one supreme fact that he is here—and must live and work to survive. He must forever climb mysterious heights beyond his present level. And always they seem elusive, unreachable, unknowable.

He very forcibly senses his existence as a living being but he sees no meaning to existence. He intuitively feels that he has a destiny and purpose for which he is forever groping along the tortuous road that leads out of the dark of his early beginnings, to the unknown Light of his seeking. All down the ages life has begun in the dark of not knowing the great secret of man's Oneness, and identity with God. Even though he may have been told of it, the telling had no meaning. The path ahead was still as dark, and as bewildering.

In this crucial hour of world danger, these vital questions of the identity and purpose of man must now be known, and fully comprehended. To remain in ignorance

of the meaning of man, and his high place in the unfolding of God's supreme Idea, is holding each man back
who is not aware of it. It is, likewise, retarding the progress of the whole human race from discovering its divine
destiny.

Before answering these vital questions I say to you in
all earnestness that new knowledge, based upon new concepts, and written in a necessarily new language, is not
a book for casual or light reading. All new knowledge
requires great mental effort. It would be impossible to
acquire more than a small percentage of what is herein
written in one reading. It is a book for a lifetime study,
not for a day.

It is not written to entertain but rather to inspire
those who are ready for the next vital stage in man's
unfolding. We are at the threshold of the Cosmic Age
wherein man will begin to recognize his divine relationship to the Creator and his Oneness with all Creation.
To attain such knowledge is to attain power to command
one's body and one's destiny. *That supreme goal is well
worth supreme effort.* Those who are ready for it will
make that effort, just as one who has a great desire to
be the head of a large industrial plant, or a concert
pianist, will make that effort with love as his motivating
force.

Let me recall to your Mind the fact that everyone
can reach the highest goal in life if he desires to and is
willing to make the effort. Those who are willing to make
the effort will find that genius is self-bestowed while the
unwilling ones will find that failure is self-inflicted. Every
child has consummate genius in him at birth. What he
does with his divine inheritance is dependent upon the
intensity of his desire to express himself. That is why the

answers to these three great human questions are so necessary for your comprehension.

Question. Who am I?

Answer. You are a divine, immortal, invisible Soul. You center a visible, physical body which consists solely of thought-waves of motion, created for the *purpose* of manifesting your divinity. Your divine immortal Soul is ONE with the Creator of the Universe. That is what Jesus meant when He said: "I and My Father are One," and "What I am, ye also are."

Many have told us these facts, but because man thinks of his body as *himself,* he has found it difficult to accept the idea of his own divinity. This fact is not difficult to accept by the few who have already been illumined from within. These few know God within them. These are the ones who have heard the Silent Voice of their Souls whispering to them in rhythms which finally had meaning. There are many today who walk and talk and work knowingly with God—and God works with them to make their work masterly. These who have learned to manifest God on earth, have reinspired others to know their divinity. They commune with God in moment to moment awareness of Him, and are the few who uplift the many, showing them the way out of the dark into the Light.

Your body is not *you. You* are the spiritual Intelligence of the ONE Mind of the Creator of all things, which centers your body as a seat of Consciousness. Within your Soul is the desire to create a body in the form of your imagining. *That is why you eventually become what you think.*

Your Soul is one of the innumerable conscious thought-centers of God's Mind universe. From that conscious thought-center of Universal Mind, your body unfolds to express thought by action, then refolds within the Soul-center for rest and renewal, before again unfolding.

Your body disappears into your Soul as completely as sound disappears into the silence from which it emerged. The rest period of your body, which disappears into your Soul between death and rebirth, is like the rest period of sleep at night between days—the only difference being in length of time. These rest periods between actions are characteristic of all effects of motion in Nature.

That is the answer to the eternal question: *Where do we go when we die?*

Our bodies go back into our Selves, from which they emerged. All bodies are but wave vibrations of motion. They spring from the universal rest condition known as the universal equilibrium and return to the invisible stillness of that equilibrium from which they sprang. The body of the oak tree arises from the stillness of its seed and refolds into its seed for rebirth. Waves of water spring into motion from their calm surface. When waves "die" they return to rest in that calm surface. These creations appear and you can see them, count them, measure them. They then disappear so you can no longer see them, count them or measure them, but they continually reappear and disappear forever. This is the life-death principle which will be clarified by numerous examples all through this book to clear away the question that bewilders the world regarding the "after death" mystery.

Your Soul is eternal. *You* are your Soul. In *you* is eternal life. The eternal *you* is never created in body form; therefore, *you* cannot die.

Your Soul is the generator of power which motivates your physical body, and it is the seat of Intelligence and

Consciousness, which creates and controls your body.

Your Soul is the "kingdom of heaven," which Jesus, God's divine Messenger, bade you to seek *within* you.

The more you know about your Soul's relation to your body, the more you will know about the intimate closeness of God to you. For this reason the vague ideas and theories concerning the Soul must be replaced by dynamic knowledge.

Many believe that the Soul is limited to human beings. They think animals do not have Souls. The idea of trees, flowers, insects, or the elements of matter having Souls is not generally accepted. It is a fact, however, that every created thing in this universe has a Soul, no matter whether it is animal, vegetable or mineral; or whether it is a complex body or simple particle of iron, calcium or silver.

Your Soul is your Mind. Both mean the same thing. *Mind* created all things so Mind centers all things it creates. Mind creates many different ideas into body forms, however, and each idea has a different pattern. Your Soul governs the pattern of the idea of man. You unfold from your Soul into the body of a man. Then you refold into your Soul to again be born as the pattern of a man. The Soul of a dog unfolds as a dog, and the Soul of a rose unfolds as the rose idea. In other words Soul means desire of Mind to divide the One Whole Idea of Creation into many ideas.

There is but one universal Soul, as there is but one universal Mind, but when you say: "My Soul," or "My Mind," you mean your identity as a unit of Creation. You think of yourself as John Doe, an individual man. There are millions of men but there is only one idea of man, or dog, or oak or violet, as species. God's Mind created all of these, but Soul in Mind governs and controls the unfolding and refolding of species. *The Soul is the record of each pattern in a body.*

To illustrate my meaning, think of an acorn. In the center of that acorn is the Soul of what can unfold into a fifty-ton oak tree, because the Soul of the oak has unfolded and refolded that particular pattern for millions of years. It has governed and controlled that unfolding idea of the oak from its beginning as a simple spore, or mold, until it became a mighty oak. Likewise, your Soul has governed and controlled the unfolding of your body from your single cell beginning. The Soul of the oak is only a microscopic point in that acorn, yet in that microscopic weightless point is every branch, leaf and root of that fifty-ton tree, yet you cannot see any part of it, even through an electronic microscope.

The Soul has the same meaning in relation to Mind as the seed has in relation to species of growing things. You would not go into a farm supply store and ask for a package of tomato Souls, you would ask for tomato seeds. However, both mean the same thing.

You know that the visible oak emerges from the invisible seed, or, more properly speaking, the oak emerges from its invisible Soul which centers its seed. You know also that as the oak unfolds from its Soul it refolds back into its Soul. By this I mean that as oaks unfold from acorns they refold their oak-tree patterns back into acorns to continue the desire of the oak-tree Soul. You may not have thought of it that way, but that is the way Nature works.

The seeds which grow on the tree are the records of the visible, living tree which has refolded its entire body pattern into the invisible Soul from which it emerged. Unfolding and refolding are simultaneous. Living and "dying" are simultaneous. There is no death, however, for the living tree still lives in its Soul-seed and will again emerge from its invisible Soul to again live as the mighty visible oak.

Death is always balanced with life. As one ceases the other becomes.

This may be new thinking to you, but it is vitally important for you to realize that you cannot die, either as a species or as an individual unit of a species. The record of YOU exists forever and eternally. Your body unfolded its patterned form from your eternal Soul and it refolded its patterned form, and every thought and action of your life, back into your Soul. That is God's bookkeeping and recording system. It is also the expansion-contraction principle of electric action and reaction which performs the work of unfolding patterned bodies from the invisible universe to make them visible, then refolding them to their invisible state.

It is also the thinking principle which concentrates to focus conceived ideas into body forms, then decentrates to rest. The body forms then disappear to rest for an interval in their invisible Souls, before again emerging to manifest the idea they symbolize by going into action again.

The visible seed which surrounds the Soul may burn up or decay, but the Soul which centers it cannot be destroyed. In that Soul is the desire for creation which cannot be voided by any condition of matter. Not even the hot fires of the sun can affect it. That identity which is enfolded there will find its condition for unfolding in another body.

The difficulty of thinking of a multitude of Souls as being separate Souls for each body might disappear by relating the idea of separate waves of the ocean to the source of all its waves. There is but one body of water in the ocean, but there are countless waves. The waves are many, but they *are* that one ocean. Likewise, there is but One Universal Mind, but all of its divided units *are* that One Mind. Also there are billions of cells in your body, but they *are* your one body.

Science has long said: "Matter seems to emerge from space and then be swallowed up by space." They still doubt, however, that the process of emergence and disappearance can be solved. The solution is simple. Bodies are electric. Mind *thinking* is electric. All electric bodies are recorded in electrical records which are stored in the invisible universe of Mind, as sound records are stored between playings.

When you desire to reproduce an electric record you place the record on the electric recorder and turn on the current. *Soul records are reborn in the same manner.* The electric power of the universal generator is "turned on" by placing the Soul-seed in the womb of mother earth, or mother body, and the record repeats itself.

All bodies emerge from the Soul and return to it. The visible emerges from the invisible, is controlled by it, and returns to it. That is the answer to the question: *Where do I go when I die? You* never die. The visible body of you which emerged from the invisible *you* returns to *you*. It returns to your Soul for rebirth for ever and ever until your separate "individuality" is lost in One Being, as individual waves are lost in one ocean.

When you have finally reached the stage of complete unity with your God-Self you will become One with God and lose your desire to manifest individuality. However, this state may be thousands of lives ahead for it is the Ultimate.

CHAPTER III

What Am I?

Question. What am I?

Answer. You are an individual expression of Intelligence. You are an invisible entity, centering a visible body, which is your instrument for expressing your Self. Your individuality is the sum total of every thought you have ever had since your beginning as a single cell of protoplasm, which desired to be a bigger and better cell.

It is commonly believed that the visible body is the individual entity, instead of the invisible Intelligence which centers, and controls it. Therefore, it is imperative to fully understand the relationship between the two. Whatever your body is *you* are the cause of it. Material bodies cannot even grow, or live and die, or decay of themselves alone. You cannot even lift your little finger without desire telegraphed to it *by* your Intelligence, through your brain, along a nerve wire.

Your body is but a "carbon copy" of your own dictation. It is the product of your own creation. Whatever there is in your body, your *thinking* has put there. If you listen to a tape recording of your voice and find it interrupted by a cough or sneeze, you know that you put that cough or sneeze into it. People are seemingly totally unaware that emotions of sorrow, frustration, worry, anger, fear, unkindness or any other inharmonious thought, will as automatically be recorded in their bodies as the cough or sneeze is recorded on their tape recorder. That is why people often say when illness afflicts them, "How can this happen to me?" They never realize that somewhere at some time they, themselves, have either planted the seed for it by their own thinking or by the many causes outside of themselves in their environment from which no human can completely immunize himself.

Your *personality* is what you cause it to be. You have complete control over that. Your *body* is what your limited control makes it become but your environment very strongly affects your ability to completely control it. Your power of control is measured by your knowledge. You have probably never thought of that.

Outside environment shares control with you in such ills as colds, malaria, typhus and other contagions, but the so-called degenerative diseases, such as cancer, stomach ulcers, tumors, and heart disease are completely under your control and therefore self-inflicted. Knowledge of their cause, however, will give you the power to cancel them by reversal of the process which created them. Two complete chapters are devoted to this subject later.

We even give names to our bodies with the belief that the body named Anna or John is the individual person. We do not give thought to the invisible Soul which is the Source of our individuality. Individuality means separateness, or the difference in personalities. We see the difference in people only through the manifestations of their thoughts as they express them in action. For that reason it is quite natural that we attribute the individuality to the body.

All individuals have different desires. Their thoughts express their desires. The body automatically records the image of their desires. The individual who would think inventive thoughts differs from the individual who would be satisfied on an assembly line. The assembly-line worker does not look like the inventor. His thoughts would create a different type. Each individual becomes what he thinks.

No two people have ever thought the same combination of thoughts. That is why there can be no two individuals who are exactly alike. A man who loves the works of Shakespeare, Tennyson, Beethoven, Mozart and Raphael has an entirely different individuality from one whose desires run to murder stories, detective stories, prize fights or other sensuous pleasures. You cannot see the thoughts or desires of either of these two individuals but you can observe their personalities.

Every individual expresses his personality through everything he does, whether it is a visible or invisible action. A personality can be judged by his postures and gestures—by his actions alone and in public—his reaction when he wins or loses a game—his appreciation or lack of interest in cultural things—his generosity, friendliness or selfishness and a host of other visible evidences of his character.

There are countless invisible evidences, however, such as the way he expresses himself in letters—how he answers the telephone or words a telegram. Even his handwriting gives strong evidence of his innate individuality.

All these visible and invisible evidences are proof that no man can avoid revealing his thoughts to his fellowman.

The individual whose desire is prize fighting or wrestling makes the type of body which tells the world what kind of individual he is. No one would mistake him for a poet or a typist. Likewise, the man who desires to be a runner will make his body into the lithe form of a runner.

Very few people realize that their thoughts and desires

are immediately stamped on their faces and bodies. A happy individual, who has a high sense of humor, attracts others to him. The corners of his mouth turn upward and his eyes twinkle in friendliness. Such an individual makes many friends because he has friendly thoughts and de· sires. He attracts people by the happy individuality which he has stamped upon his body.

Every portrait painter who studies the face he is paint- ing can clearly see his sitter's emotional history. The sit- ter's whole life seems to gradually unfold before him. Very often his or her selfish or frustrated thoughts are so vividly stamped upon the face that the painter finds it necessary to drive such thoughts away by interjecting happy thoughts.

When anyone applies for a position he creates either a pleasant or unpleasant impression at once. That impres- sion is not given by his present thoughts, for one might assume a happy attitude to give a pleasant impression. The keen eye and intuition of the experienced personnel manager gathers a life impression at first glance, which may tell him to not employ this one, or to employ that one. He intuitively knows a strong or weak character, one he could or could not trust, or one who has initiative to whom he could give responsibility, or one who would watch the clock with eagerness for closing time.

Every dramatic school stresses the necessity for its stu- dents to actually think the thought of the characters they are impersonating, even when not speaking. The audi- ence must see you think, they say. You must become your character. You must show fear, anger or other emotions every second while acting them. Your very body gestures change with every emotion, just as your face changes. You can see by this illustration that the body is not the individual who acts through it. A good actor, who may be a very gentle individual, can impersonate a murderer by sending a different combination of thoughts through his body, to make his body manifest a different individuality from his own.

Is it not clear to you, therefore, that your body is only a canvas upon which you are painting your own portrait? An artist can paint the portraits of many different individuals upon the same canvas, or an actor can make his body express many types of individuals, by temporarily thinking another combination of thoughts. You can also transform yourself permanently into a higher type of individual by thinking other thoughts than you have been thinking.

If you wish to transform your individuality into a greater one, begin thinking great thoughts, beautiful thoughts, powerful and friendly thoughts, and your personality will immediately reflect your changed thinking. Your face will have a different expression in every detail, as well as your whole bearing. Your very posture and gestures will mark you as a transformed being. You will even walk differently. A criminal does not walk the way a scholar walks, nor are his postures and gestures the same. The criminal shows fear in his walk if he is hunted, or he slinks and crouches, instead of walking erect as the man of noble character does.

You can become what you want to become and your very aura will tell the world what standard of Intelligence the Individual is whom your body impersonates. There are no limits which you cannot reach if your desires are great enough. Your being will always tell of your greatness and the standard of individual you are.

A good example of this fact is a body of a piano. It

cannot make a sound of itself, but when a great master musician expresses his thoughts through it, the world knows that a great individual Intelligence controls that body. Conversely, a sensuous individual will extend his physical sensuousness through that same piano body, and the world will know that an entirely different type of individual controls it.

Consider the effect of each individual upon the human race as a whole. One uplifts the whole world culturally, while the other drags it down. An inspired genius reinspires others to great heights of spiritual ecstasy. He awakens the divinity in others and uplifts them to the realms of their spiritual natures, which makes them forget their bodies. The physically sensuous musician creates just the opposite effect. His jazz rhythms drag them to lower physical levels and awaken all of the physical desires of bodies. He manufactures his type of individuality.

The more knowledge you acquire of God's plan of Creation, and His processes of Creation, the more you will comprehend your power over your body. *You cannot command that which you do not know.*

Every individual acts as he believes. If what he believes is not true, however, his actions are not right actions. He hurts himself instead of helping himself. His series of actions, however, constitute his individuality, or personality. The greater your knowledge of *what you are* the greater your conscious Intelligence can build and control a body to manifest your individual Intelligence. If you desire to become what is known as a great person, first ask yourself if your thinking is directed inwardly toward your Soul-Self, or outwardly toward the objective universe through your senses.

There are only two types of individuals in the world,

however, those who think inwardly toward their spiritual Selves and those who think outwardly toward their physical senses. All people think both ways but a Mozart or Leonardo type thinks inwardly most of the time, while the masses think outwardly most of the time. A Beethoven is a spiritual individual, whose sense of values lies in giving out the abundance of his Self to the world, while a Napoleon is a physical individual whose sense of values lies in the taking of material possessions for personal aggrandizement.

The strange thing about individuality is the misconception of its meaning to the average person. The great individual is one who gradually loses his individuality as increased God-awareness in him makes him become universal. Therefore, the highest aim in life is to lose your individuality in order to attain universality. The greater the God-awareness in any man the closer he is to complete Mind-Oneness. The completed journey of life ends in the omnipotence and omniscience of man's universality with God.

CHAPTER IV

Why Am I Here?

Question. Why am I here?

Answer. You are here to manifest God, your Creator, as one unit of the idea of man. You are here to become an actor in the Cosmic Drama of Cause and Effect which the Master Playwright has conceived to express the idea of Love, upon which basis the universe is founded. That means that you are to take the very long journey of life which begins in a single cell of protoplasm. That single cell is centered by your Soul, which is your Mind-control during the long ages of building your body under the guidance and constant co-operation of your centering Soul. That journey takes millions of years of gradual transformation from physical awareness of body to spiritual awareness of Mind. The journey ends in complete universality, or Oneness with God.

The journey of the unfoldment of the man idea, which we call the human race, is divided into five stages. They are as follows:

The first stage was the primate, unmoral, instinctively controlled period of mere body building and fighting for survival. Man, the fighter and procurer of food, was supreme. Woman was only considered man's chattel and slave. This stage ended at the dawn of Consciousness.

The second stage is the present pagan, or barbarian sense-dominated stage. It is the beginning of awareness between right and wrong, and the elevation of woman to an ever-increasing importance, but never of sufficient importance to create a balanced civilization. Even today it is still a man's world. Instinctive control lessens as man recognizes the unfolding of Mind and exercises free will. This barbarian stage is characterized by greed for material possessions and power over others, which it acquired by might-over-right practices. This barbarian stage will continue as long as man kills man, believes in evil and suppresses woman to less than full equality with man.

The third stage is the Mind-dominated first stage of Consciousness, or the genius period. It is the second moral period of higher ideals and greater God-awareness. It is also the first stage where man knowingly becomes co-creator with God by being able to transfer invisible Mind idea into visible body forms. The genius fully comprehends the rhythms of God's language and interprets those rhythms for other men. The barbarian and the genius stages overlap, for there have already been several hundred geniuses among the billions of barbarians. During the genius stage the idea of evil almost entirely disappears.

The fourth stage is the Cosmic Conscious period of unfolding. It is the higher moral and spiritual stage of complete God-awareness. This period is distinctly marked by the disappearance of instinctive control, sense of evil and forgetfulness of body. It is the stage of the mystic who is almost fully omniscient and omnipotent. Twenty or thirty humans have already reached this high stage.

The fifth stage is Christ Consciousness, or complete awareness of unity with God. This is the final stage of universality, omniscience and omnipotence in man. In the Christ Conscious being Love has been fully manifested on earth and evil has fully disappeared. One man only has ever reached this final stage of all men.

In order to better comprehend the plan of life and man's purpose on earth we will review the five stages in more detail.

PRIMATE MAN

First stage. The man idea begins with the slow building of a body when the planet spirals far enough away from the sun to have prepared the conditions which are necessary for the unfoldment of human life.

The first cycles of man's life start with a few minutes duration and increase in duration over a period of millions of years as desire for a body adds more and more cells. Single cells first divide into male and female opposites by the polarizing power of the electric current of Nature. As cells multiply, however, their ever complexing patterns must be recorded in the Soul-seed record.

Life cycles gradually lengthen by that complexing and recording process until the life cycle nears eighty years. The period of gestation has also lengthened from a few minutes to nine months. Everything the body needs to fulfill its desires it borrows from the earth and returns every milligram of those borrowings to the earth when it can no longer function as a body. Desire gradually creates all bodies cell by cell. Body unfoldment keeps pace with desire for body.

As desire adds new parts and new abilities, each new part, which is extended from its center of control, must be "wired" to that center in order that it may be operated from its centering Intelligence. That which we call *wiring* in an electric machine made by man, we call *sensing* in

living organic machines created by God. The senses of
the body are two-way message carriers to all parts of the
body from the Mind *through* the brain and back again.

It is commonly supposed that we have five senses, hearing, feeling, tasting, smelling and seeing. We have but
one sense, however, *the sense of feeling*. We feel through
our eyes, our ears, our palate, our bodies and our nostrils.
The one sense of feeling is the vibration of the electric
current as it passes through our nerves. That sense of
electric vibration is the only thing which makes the body
aware of its existence. When the body is electrically
charged it has an electrical awareness of body existence.
Without sufficient electrical charge in a body to send
vibration impulses along its wires it has no sense of
existence. That is what happens when one sleeps.

As the body extends in complexity and mass, its centering seat of sensation, which we call the brain, also enlarges its two growing electric battery cells which act
as "self-starters" for body activities. This two-lobe electric
storage battery, which the brain is, has no knowledge
whatsoever. It is no more related to Intelligence than
one's fingernail. The seat of Intelligence, or Mind, or
Soul, is located in the pituitary gland. When Mind thinks,
it expresses its desires electrically through the brain when
the body batteries are sufficiently charged to motivate the
brain. Very few people *think* with their Mind, however.
They *sense* with their *brain* by releasing its stored-up
records which we call memories. The entire office of the
brain is to receive, transmit and record sensations when
it has sufficient electrical charge to operate the body machine.

All storage batteries run down, however. Human, animal and vegetable storage batteries become completely

discharged daily. They become like the "dead batteries" of your car. Being unable to send messages to other parts of the body the senses lose all of their electrical awareness. The body loses all sense of existence for a period of several hours every day. When our electric batteries thus become discharged we say that we are asleep. When our heartbeat renews its power to "charge our batteries," we say we are awake.

We also say other things which are not true to Nature's plan. We say that we are unconscious. We use that word in the sense that implies our Consciousness ceases. *Our Consciousness is our immortal, eternal Intelligence.* That never ceases.

Mind Intelligence is always conscious but the *thinking* of Mind is electric. Electricity is divided into action and rest periods which we call cycles. One half of every electric cycle starts from rest and extends into multiplied action. This could be likened to a man awakening from rest and working hard all day. The other half divides the power for action and returns to rest, as a man does when he can no longer work and must rest. That is the life-death principle of electric bodies. To live they must start from rest in their seed to grow into action. To die they must reverse the process and decay into rest in their seed. Consciousness has no life-death cycles. Consciousness belongs to the immortality of Mind. It is eternally changeless.

The misconception of the so-called state of unconsciousness is based on the premise that the brain is the Mind, instead of being only a "switchboard" through which the Mind can think, or the senses can operate when it is sufficiently charged. That which is really the Conscious Mind is what is presumed to be the "subconscious"

Mind. There is no subconscious Mind. Mind is not strati-
fied. There is only Mind at rest, and Mind in action—
which means *thinking*.

When you sleep, thinking you are unconscious, your
Intelligence is as wide awake as it always is, but you have
turned off the electric current which allows *you* to think
or sense through your body. You will comprehend this
better if you step into your car and press the self-starter
button. Nothing happens. You say that its batteries are
dead. You do not say that it is asleep. Neither do you say
it is unconscious. You are the conscious Intelligence
which centers and controls the motivation of your car
but you cannot move it. If you "awaken it" by charging
its batteries for ten minutes, it will move a little, but it
will not have full power to move until fully charged.
Likewise, you can awaken a man who has slept only a
short time and he can move, but he could not fulfill a
normal day of activity until he has "caught up with his
sleeping," which means until his batteries have been fully
recharged.

This misconception about subconscious and supercon-
scious Mind is a deterrent to the principle which says:
"Man know thyself," which is necessary for mankind in
order that he can steer his ship through the complex dangers of the sea of life.

During man's whole first stage he builds his body and
fights for its survival by instinctive control from his centering Soul. He has no will of his own. He merely obeys
the electric messages sent through his nerve wiring and
he obeys these commands as automatically as a stone falls
directly toward the center of gravity. When a telegram is
sent through a wire, the wire has no comprehension whatsoever of the idea contained in the message. Neither does

primate man have any idea of the commands which are sent through his senses. He merely lives and obeys his instincts the way birds, insects and other living bodies obey.

As he continues to obey he builds his body and adds constantly to it. He constantly transforms his body as his brain enlarges to meet its complexing needs. His slanting forehead straightens, his crouching body stands erect, and his massive jaws grow smaller. During this entire period he has no creative faculty whatsoever. He can reason somewhat with his senses but he never even created a boat, nor a sail, wheel or fire until after the dawn of Mind-awareness in him. Likewise, he had no moral sense, either of good or evil, until Consciousness first dawned in him, which was only about fifteen thousand years ago in man's history.

During the entire primate period woman had no place of importance in man's life other than as a chattel. Man fought for family survival. Survival, and fighting for it, was the thing of first import. Nothing else counted. The primate world was entirely a man's world.

PAGAN-BARBARIAN MAN

The second stage of man's unfolding is the pagan, or barbarian age—which we are now in. It began when the first faint suspicion of a higher power than man entered his Consciousness. He then began to think, to reason, to discover flame, the boat, the sail for the boat and the wheel. The idea of morality dawned in his unfolding awareness. He divided right from wrong. There was good and evil. He began to command matter by knowing about matter. He commanded the earth to yield harvests for him, and made implements to multiply his command. Woman worked with him in the ground. She raised his sheep, his goats, his cattle. She made tents and raiment. Woman began to be important in man's esteem—instead of only in his life.

The forever search for the great unknown led to sun worship, demon worship, idol worship. Man then made gods of wood—of stone—man-gods—always *man*-gods, made in man's image for man.

Long centuries passed, then the One God was envisioned by man. He still remained the male God made in the image of man, for man. Man made Him to be like man, to be pleased with the shedding of blood, to be wrathful, vengeful and quick to anger. Men worshiped their male God of wrath at altars drenched with blood. Tens of thousands of sheep, goats and bullocks were slain to appease God in hope of remission of sins. Neophytes were drenched with overflowing fountains of blood at their baptismal ceremonials.

Heroic pagan legends told of the pleasure given to their One God of wrath by some hero who slew a thousand men with the jawbone of an ass, and similar heroic stories conceived by barbarians who still remembered their primate days, and still loved bloodshed, slaughter and conquest of man by man.

Great civilizations grew and fell again and again—each time to arise a little higher and again fall. Relics and monuments remained above the earth to tell of these civilizations—pyramids, and temples, and tombs, in Egypt, in the high Andes, in Yucatan, in Tibet and India. Evil became a reality as man thought evil and practiced it. Evil became legendary. Magic, the supernatural, the unnatural and the miraculous formed the basis of thousands of pagan legends about evil and the reality of evil.

The most damaging of these pagan legends to human progress is that monstrous legend which would have you believe that a serpent could have intelligent conversation with a woman—that a serpent had knowledge of good and evil—that good and evil grew on a tree—and that evil came into the world because a man ate an apple. The viciousness of the legend lies in the assumption that the evil and sin of the world is God's holy law of mating which unites fathers and mothers of Creation into one so that they can again create more fathers and mothers to continue God's plan. It made our God of Love to be the Creator of evil. This legend of evil created evil itself by being one of the causes of plunging all that is good in man into twelve centuries of bestial sex degradation. It bred cruelties and tortures of two inquisitions.

Countless thousands of people still believe this early pagan legend which typifies the stage of gross ignorance of the world of that day. It demonstrates how difficult it is for man to escape from his own primacy. These legends have become tradition to man, which means that he believes things unthinkingly because he has always believed them, so he no longer subjects them to logical reasoning. Such beliefs hold mankind back by retarding the unfolding of his higher spiritual nature. *Just so long as man prefers to be pagan by insisting upon pagan beliefs and practices, he will still be pagan.* Man is always what he thinks. He cannot become spiritually exalted by being physically depraved or by thinking depravity.

Pagan memories are still interwoven into our enlightenment of today as tradition, and tradition is strong because it is repeated unthinkingly. We even unthinkingly sing pagan traditional hymns. We sing: "There is a fountain filled with blood drawn from Immanuel's veins, and sinners plunged beneath that flood lose all their guilty stains." That hymn would have been appropriate for a pagan baptismal festival where dozens of live animals were slaughtered to appease the bestial God of their own bestial conceiving, but not for gatherings of gentle people who would shudder with terror at such a scene.

It takes many centuries of higher civilizations to eliminate the traditional beliefs of our early pagan days in which devils, demons, evil spirits and other superstitions of that day's gross ignorance are still carried into this day. As long as our beliefs are pagan, our civilization will be pagan.

God sent Mind-illumined messengers to hasten the unfoldment of man's spiritual nature—the Buddha, Zoroaster, Moses, Confucius, Lao-tzu and Jesus to tell of the One God of Love, but tradition was stronger than truth. The male God of wrath and fear persisted in their day and still persists in ours. For instance we still continue to say: "We are a nation of God-*fearing* men" whereas we should say: "We are a nation of God-*loving* men." The roots of dead beliefs are hard to uproot, but man must suffer until they are rooted out of him. He must suffer by living in the world of his own making, and the kind of world he makes is the kind of man he is.

Man-thinking created the warring world of fear, hatred, enmity and disunity we are forced to live in today. Man made it in his own likeness—in his own male-thinking image. Genghis Khan made the world of his day in his own image. Then came Alexander, Caesar, Charlemagne, Frederick and Peter the Great, Ivan the Terrible, William the Conqueror, Napoleon, Bismarck, Hitler, Lenin, Stalin, Mussolini. and other male conquerors, tyrants, dictators, marauding bands of Huns, Tartars, Manchus, Norsemen and other terrorists who have made the world over repeatedly in their male images.

Woman slowly rose in man's esteem in parts of the world. Wherever woman made her influence felt as the spiritual mate of her physical man, nations responded to that influence and progressed with great rapidity. Wherever woman was suppressed, however, that nation retrogressed. It could not keep up with world flow. *The measure in which any country has progressed is the measure of its recognition of woman.* Man still thinks of himself as master in his own house. He still thinks of his own mental superiority as ruler of world-government and world-business. He still thinks of a woman as a cook and homemaker. When women organized to fight for equal suffrage rights men thought of it as an utter absurdity. But when man's wars made it imperative for woman to share in manufacture and industry, she excelled men in many capacities even though it was all new thinking for her.

Man's seemingly total ignorance of God's plan concerning the man-woman mate relationship, has made him unaware that He created man and woman as equal halves of *one,* for unity is impossible between two unequal halves. Man, the marauder, the fighter, the conqueror, has had millions of years to remember his life-destroying days of killing to take happiness away from others. Woman, the mother, the giver of life, has had millions of years to remember the service she has given to man.

The spiritual love nature of woman has never had a chance of balancing the progress of civilization and, for that reason, civilizations have repeatedly fallen as our present civilization must inevitably fall because of its

own unbalance and disunity in all of the essentials neces-
sary for a normal existence.

For thousands of years the pagan-barbarian civilization remained at a very low unchanging level. About
eight hundred years ago a greater spiritual awakening
advanced man to an ever-increasing level. Steadily gather-
ing momentum it progressed the human race farther intellectually in the last one hundred years than in previous
thousands of years. During the last eight hundred years,
painting and music, and literature, the greatest of the
spiritually transforming arts, came into being. Sculpture
and architecture had been here before. These are the
static arts which did not reach to the Soul of early man.
The rhythms of music and painting express the meter of
man's heartbeat and the universal heartbeat. They have
the power to reach the Soul through their dynamism,
which sculpture and architecture lacked.

The diatonic scale in music was unknown to man until
one hundred years after Leonardo lived. Caesar never
knew the divine music which is ours to know. The human
Consciousness had not unfolded in that day to the stage
where it would have meaning. A Bach, Beethoven or
Wagner rendition would have been but boring noise to
a Caesar or Nero, just as it still is to a prize fighter or any
lover of bloodshedding sports today. An age of paganism
which gloried in gladiatorial fights, one in which the
greatest pleasure of women and children was in witness-
ing lions rend humans, or bloodshed of man by man in
the arenas of that day, could not possibly have understood
our tonal music had they had it.

Music, however, was the greatest cause of bringing love
into the human race. As the music, painting and sculpture

of the great masters came into the world, cruelty and
blood-lust went out of it. The rhythmic beat of all great
music, and the tonal harmonies of all great art, interprets
the universal heartbeat. It reaches man's Soul by inducing
inner thinking to replace outer sensing. Inner thinking
is meditative and gives birth to desire for prayer and
prayer is an innate and intuitive desire to talk to God.

The growth of music awakened the spiritual in man
and inspired in him the urge to find God. Music and
worship are synonymous. Each is the other. The Christian spirit rose from its ashes and uplifted man one step
higher upon his long climb. It was but a little step higher
but it transformed the human race.

The power of the newly awakened Christian spirit in
the first spiritual rebirth of this barbarian age brought
world-culture and its consequent higher stage of human
friendliness up to the standard which gave us the eight
great centuries of progress, which we are now about to
lose. It did not bring knowledge, however. Man's concepts
are still pagan. His concept of God is still a great powerful
man with a physical body and a great capacity to wrath.
Human understanding is not yet unfolded to the point
where it can comprehend power and love in an invisible
God, even though the greatest power known to man is
gravity, and gravity is invisible. Nor can the pagan Mind
comprehend heaven being anywhere but above the earth
among the clouds where good people ascend to when they
die. Pagan concepts inherited from pagan legends and
superstitions prevent Christian practice from advancing
at the same pace as Christian spirit, as indicated by the
steady rise of world-culture.

*Christian spirit without Christian practice will never
make a Christian world.* The ultimate of a Christian

world is the unity and peace which comes from knowledge of God's ways and practices. It means one-world-unity in brotherly love and obedience to God's One Law of rhythmic balanced interchange in all man's transactions with man, as Nature observes that law in her transactions.

Spiritual culture rose steadily for centuries, but barbaric greed and primate memories of blood and conquest in the masses, were not eliminated sufficiently to balance the spiritual growth which was transforming the few. Spiritual growth, however, was sufficiently strong in man to give birth to an electric age which completely transformed world-thinking and living conditions. Our past hundred years of progress have been greater than all of the centuries preceding it since the days of the Renaissance.

By the year 1900 man had gained the whole world at the price of his Soul. During all these centuries, while the Silent Voice had been awakening the divine spark in countless thousands of Souls, the masses preferred to continue their barbarian practices.

Today the mass-barbarian is syncopating the universal rhythms of the great masters into the jungle rhythms of their understanding. The high point of scientific advancement is now an integral part of the huge man-killing industry which man has set up in his man-built world, instead of the Golden Rule, "Love ye one another" world, which is the basis of the Christian spirit.

As love again goes out of the world, ugliness and brutality are coming into it in all human culture, as in all human practice. As the culture loving people of the Hellenic age saw its beautiful sculptures thrown into the seas, so do the culture loving people of today see the ugliness of modern art gradually infiltrating even our art museums, and the jazz of jungle rhythms displace our gracious minuet and our happy Viennese waltz. Even the musical instruments which have the capacity of reaching the Soul through their likeness to Nature's sounds, are being discarded from all but the symphony orchestras and replaced with noisy brass instruments to please the ever-increasing decadence of the masses.

The poetic quality of musical rendition is being replaced with raucous noise more reminiscent of the jungle than of gentility. The violin, flute and piccolo are suggestive of whispering winds, the songs of birds, the reedy sounds of insects, and the humming, droning, buzzing and chirping sounds of wood life. The soft, dreamy, restful dinner music of the 1900 era, which lent inspiration to social gatherings, has been replaced with ear splitting brass horns in dining rooms, night clubs and television. The rhythmic harmonies of our fast disappearing cultural age are no longer heard. In their stead as much discord as possible is introduced into syncopated melodies to destroy all that is fine and uplifting in this greatest of the spiritual arts.

Cultural degradation is always paralleled by sex degradation, sex perversion and a fast lowering of the moral code. Every falling civilization follows this same pattern of growing sex bestiality which multiplies as culture lowers and the fine arts disappear from their thrones. The increase of sex perversion in Greece kept pace with its death of culture. This pattern is again repeating itself in our own rapidly falling civilization. All forms of sex perversion are rapidly increasing even among the children of our present age. Sex perversion leads very rapidly to the jungle and awakens, even in children, the desire to kill. *Over and over again the world is shocked by youth killings for sheer pleasure.* The world attributes these events to youth delinquency. Instead of that they are the fruit of world-decadence. Delinquency is not confined to youth alone. There is marked delinquency in every walk of life. The rapid increase in crime by adult delinquents more than matches the degradation of our youth.

The matter which should greatly concern our present day intellectuals is the fact that each succeeding generation of youths will be born into a lower moral status of civilization. Eventually all that is fine in the human race will not even be a memory for centuries, except among the few who keep the Light burning between these dark periods in monasteries or secluded places. The spiritually exalted ones kept the Light burning during the dark ages until the rebirth of civilization in the 14th century.

Unless we immediately begin to transform the human race to a man-*for*-man basis to replace the present man-*against*-man basis, the human race is as certain to fall again as it has so many times fallen in the past for the same reason. If this does happen there are more of the spiritually illumined among us to carry the Light over the dark intervening centuries than there were during the last fall of man. Even these would find life hard, difficult and dangerous. They would have to live very secluded lives in remote mountain wildernesses, and very probably in high-walled castles of mediaeval architecture to protect their groups from marauding bandits in the lawless centuries which would follow.

Crime and youth delinquency have brought such moral degradation to the world that thinking people are now saying that only a great spiritual awakening can save the world. A spiritual awakening is impossible which does not conform with spiritual laws. Spiritual teachings which do not conform with God's law can be likened to the desires of a man who wished to be good, happy and peaceful but acquired money for that purpose by burglary, larceny and cruelty.

The foregoing is an excellent picture of our man-made world since its first spiritual resurrection in the 14th century. This could not have happened had man and woman grown *equally* in the building of our civilization. It is quite probable that the human race could have found the enduring peace for which it was searching within another hundred years, if it had not been forced to reap the harvest of enmity and hate, which empire builders had sown into the world-pattern.

This is a great pity, for the world is on the eve of a greater hundred years than our last one hundred. The electronic age, which is now in the making, will make our present miracle world seem quite primitive. This promised unfolding will be impossible to build against the resistance of the present world-retrogression toward ever multiplying disunity.

We have not been permitted that extra one hundred years of peace which would have probably led to the equalization of man and woman in government affairs. We are now beginning to put this equalization into practice, however, for men no longer think of it as being ridiculous for women to occupy high seats in industry and government. Had man and woman worked equally together in these past hundred years the return to man-killing would undoubtedly not have happened and we would not now be facing the terrible harvest of past man-killings.

We have prayed for happiness, peace and prosperity for ourselves, while plundering our neighbor to take his peace, happiness and prosperity away from him. *Unknowingly we have actually done to ourselves what we have done to our neighbor.* We built the image of ourselves into our empires—and they tumbled like a house of cards. In killing a million sons of neighbors, we killed ten million of our own sons. For each billion dollars plundered to enrich us, we are impoverished by ten billion dollars of debts.

We did not know what we were doing. We were immoral pagans working according to the pattern of our barbarian nature as truly and as normally as primate man acted in the pattern of his true primate nature. Ignorance of the law does not excuse us, however. It never does. We shall continue to live in a barbarian world of our own making as long as we practice barbarian ways. We have not yet known man, nor God, sufficiently to comprehend our close relation, which necessitates co-ordination and co-operation in whatever God and man do together. Man's failure to work with God, and the penalty which he brings down upon himself for such disobedience, is plainly set down in the following quotation from The Message of the Divine Iliad:

"Serve first thy brother. Hurt first thyself rather than thy neighbor. Gain nought from him unbalanced by thy giving. Protect thou the weak with thy strength, for if thou use thy strength against him his weakness will prevail against thee, and thy strength will avail thee nought."

Man has violated this law all through his barbarian days, and is still violating it while hoping to evade its consequences. Every weak nation he has conquered is today the conqueror. The very theory of conquest by war is for the purpose of *enrichment,* while the effect of every war ever fought by man is *impoverishment.* How many more times must man suffer the agonies of war before he finally knows the law by paying the price of learning his lessons through more suffering?

SUMMARY

This Barbarian Age might be briefly summed up as a sense-dominated, man-controlled age in which greed for material gain motivated man to take as much as he could get by giving as little as he could give. During its history the spiritual qualities of man began to unfold because of the birth among them of divinely inspired Messengers who came into the world to help man's unfolding. Their teachings were beyond man's comprehension but the awakening of desire for spiritual unfoldment grew strong in him. These teachings might have brought the human race to a realization of its Oneness with God, and the brotherhood of man, save for the much stronger innate memories of its primate man-killing days.

During its entire period this age has been marked with a belief in evil because of a practice of what it believed to be evil. Its most hopeful sign of progress was the rise of woman from utter insignificance to a sufficiently high place within the last fifty years to allow her to vote in man's affairs of government, which still remained man-controlled, however. That is the first step toward the necessary man-woman equalization, but it is only a very little step.

Because of these immaturities in the slowly unfolding human race its civilizations fell many times, as our civilization is now once again inevitably falling.

Let us pray that the men and women of the world will unite in time to reverse this decadence to a more glorious Renaissance than our world has ever known.

CHAPTER V

Mind Consciousness

The third stage in human unfolding is Mind Con-
sciousnes, which is the stage that follows *sense consciousness*. It is the stage represented by world geniuses.

The average man considers geniuses to be specially
born. They are not specially born, however. They are
like other men except that they are farther unfolded
spiritually. Mind Consciousness has always belonged to
man since the beginning. The human race does not
acquire new qualities. It reveals existent ones as it unfolds. Nothing is ever added to man from without. Whatever man becomes, physically, intellectually or spiritually,
unfolds from *within*. Even after millions of years of his
unfolding, all that appears was in the first cells of his
beginning. Nature does not evolve. It eternally unfolds
and refolds.

All idea is eternally existent. The man-idea is a part
of the One Whole Idea of Creation. It is complete as
IDEA but its manifestation in time and space is divided
into timed recordings in space. Likewise, all knowledge
exists in the Soul-seed of all mankind. The genius discovers this fact from much aloneness—much meditation
—much communion with Nature. He discovers that
knowledge comes in flashes of inspiration as he desires it.
When he expresses his desire by inner thinking it unfolds
within his Consciousness, and he recognizes it. He realizes
that he has always known it.

The genius knows that knowledge is limited to *un-changing cause* and cannot be acquired through *fleeting effects* of ever-changing matter, unless translated back to cause by inner thinking. Effects of motion are observed by the senses but the senses cannot acquire knowledge. The senses can record and repeat effects but cannot *know* that which they record and repeat. Knowing, therefore, that knowledge is a quality of Mind only, and cannot be sensed, and also knowing that creative energy has its existence in Mind only, geniuses acquire power to command material bodies from within their own Consciousness. The more they become aware of their own centering Consciousness, from which their knowledge and power is extended, the more they become aware of their divinity and Oneness with God. Increasing God-awareness gradually brings the ecstasy of the God-Mind and full awareness that God is forever working with them, as they work with Him to give masterliness to their creations. Works thus created endure forever. No work of man is enduring unless created in the ecstasy of God-awareness which characterizes all geniuses. All works of man, which are but the recordings and repeatings of sensed observations and memories, are but transient and fleeting. God is not in them. Man's senses alone are in them. They are Soulless. They do not inspire, for inspiration is not in them.

Men who have reached that high state of Consciousness know their destiny from early childhood. They are in full control of their destiny and would not compromise for all the wealth in the world. Once they have found the treasures of heaven within themselves they would die penniless rather than sully their creations. To them it would be an exchange of immortality for a mirage.

Every genius is aware of his exalted position as a di-

vinely inspired messenger to those who are seeking the
Light. Those thousands whom he inspires are exalted
to greater and still greater heights. The human race is
thus enriched by each inspired messenger to man who
speaks to man in God's inspired language. It is through
such messengers that culture comes into the world to
slowly uplift it to its higher stages. As culture increases
in man his ability to become inspired multiplies. *The
ascension of any man to great heights is dependent upon
his ability to become reinspired by the inspired messages
brought to him by world geniuses.* Mind multiplies his
power to uplift mankind to higher cultural levels when
he is engaged in peaceful pursuits which promote friendliness. When he is engaged in warlike pursuits and unfair
business practices which promote enmities, human progress ceases. It reverses toward decadence.

An increasing number of geniuses have come into the
world since the beginning of the 14th century, but their
number has not exceeded one hundred during the six
centuries of world progress which so suddenly ended in
the year of 1914. When the world becomes decadent it
crucifies genius. Lack of recognition and patronage prevents genius from giving its priceless treasures to the
world. In addition many lose all opportunity of enriching
the world by being compelled to kill men instead of
serve them. The measure in which inspiration is withdrawn from men is the measure in which spiritual decadence takes whole civilizations back toward their primacy.

*God will work with men who desire to work with Him,
but He will not work for men beyond their own desire.*
Decadence is more conspicuous in the great masses who
have not advanced to the point where they have the

slightest awareness of that spiritual state of Mind which inspiration is. There are countless millions of these un-inspired, unillumined human units who are still deeply barbarian.

There are many, many thousands, however, who have developed the inner vision and the inner ears, which inspiration unfolds in every man. These many thousands are the fruit of the few who have made them inwardly see and hear those concepts of imaginings, and the voices which arise from Nature's silences, that are beyond the range of physical perception. These are the ones who will save the race, if it is to be saved, but their numbers are one to one thousand, or even less. They are the few cultured ones who love a symphony concert and would suffer at a prize fight, against the countless thousands who love the prize fight, and would suffer at a symphony concert. *These are the ones who are keeping the Christian spirit alive in the world by leading man in the direction of the kingdom of heaven, which man may find only through inner inspired thinking.*

Inner thinking men seek aloneness in the forests and far reaches in Nature, away from the noises of man's activities. They thus insulate themselves from their own body desires and from all sounds which are not the rhythmic pulsations of Nature. Such aloneness leads to deep meditation and silent prayer. Aloneness invites close communion with God. He who thus seeks God will find Him. He will know Him by seeing His Light with inner vision, hearing His Voice coming out of Nature's silences in the rhythms of its heartbeat, and feeling the ecstasy of His love nature upon which His universe is based. In such great aloneness of man with God, all that is evil in primate man disappears into its own dark.

The great masters could not possibly interpret God's rhythmic language if even the slightest trace of evil touched their thinking. Likewise, no man can listen with his Soul to the rhythmic symphonies of the great masters and think evil while so listening. Herein lies the great power of music in conserving and multiplying the Christian spirit among men. Music is the greatest of all the powers used by man to bring about the state of Universal Brotherhood, which is primarily essential for a Christian civilization. Painting is the next great power for inducing inspiration which leads to inner thinking.

These statements are so liable to challenge by the unthinking, that it is necessary to recall that painting and music, such as we know them in our day, were unknown until the 12th and 15th centuries respectively. The spiritual nature of either music or painting could not unfold while the memory and love of bloodshed was so strong in the race that the greatest pleasures of its men, women and children, were gladiatorial killings and the rending of humans by lions.

Inner spiritual thinking had begun during the Hellenic age and evidenced its effect in the beauty of architecture and sculpture, but by the time Jesus was born there had been four hundred years of decadence in which bloodshed became the greatest pleasure. While the human race was in such a primate stage it could not comprehend God's rhythmic language. His cosmic language could only be comprehended and interpreted by those who were seeking the kingdom of heaven by inner spiritual thinking. This stage of human unfolding had never been reached until Leonardo and Raphael gave the world their interpretations of Nature's rhythms in the art of painting.

Perhaps it has not occurred to humanity at large that Leonardo and Raphael were the strongest force in re-awakening the Christian spirit. The Church of that day spoke to men in a language which had no meaning to them. They had no opportunity for comprehension, for Latin words conveyed no meaning to them whatsoever. Leonardo, Raphael, Michelangelo and many others spoke to the people of that day in God's language of color rhythms and forms which they did understand. Even the most lowly peasant could understand The Last Supper, or the Madonna and Child interpretations of numerous followers of Leonardo. Jesus became alive and real to them. The apostles and other figures, which to them were holy, rose before their eyes and filled them with a new hope. Every home became a religious shrine. Jesus and their blessed Virgin were in their very presence. Religious fervor rose to great heights as a reality in those days of seeming hopelessness. Paintings gave reality to their religion.

The spirit of man unfolded to some extent, even though religion was more emotional and ritual than worship. Pagan legend and superstition joined their powers with ignorant man's love of the supernatural to retard its growth. Spiritual man grew, however, against even that resistance, for even religious emotionalism led to desire, and desire for closer contact with God led to prayer, and prayer induced inner thinking. The words of the spiritual teachers of that day were full of fear and evil. The spiritual words of the divine messengers who spoke to people in form, color and electrical rhythms, had no fear or evil in them. Fear and evil have no existence in Nature.

It is impossible to estimate the value of painting and music to the spiritual unfoldment of man. When one realizes that less than one hundred men transformed thousands upon thousands of barbarian stage men into the realms of spiritual consciousness, it should help one to realize the value of every genius to the world. One Beethoven or one Leonardo is worth more in material value to mankind than the value of all the gold and real estate in the world, yet mankind crucifies genius today as he crucified Love 2,000 years ago. It is imperative that you more fully understand why there is such an incalculable power in the masterpieces of world-geniuses to transform men from sensuality to spirituality. It is equally imperative that you fully understand what is meant by "God's language," which you know as inspiration.

All down through man's long ages God has spoken to man. His Silent Voice spoke to him first as instinct, then as intuition, and then by inspiration. Inspiration is the language of rhythms which the genius as fully understands as other people understand the language of words. The final, or ultimate means of communication between man and God is the language of Light that comes to Christ Conscious man. Chap. VII—Christ Consciousness, further describes this final stage of unfolding.

World geniuses who talk to God through inspiration hear only the rhythms of Nature. These rhythms are in harmony with the universal heartbeat. They are the one-two rhythms of the electric pulsations of God's thinking. They are in tune with every action-reaction of Nature. That is what is meant by being "in tune with the Infinite." There are no unbalanced or split rhythms in spiritual Nature, such as those which sensual man makes use of for body excitation. The rhythms and attunement of falling waters, or the whisperings of soft winds in meadows, or the mighty pounding of the surf on seashore sands are in tune with the inbreathings-outbreathings of this planet or the beating of every living heart in the universe. These are the rhythms which the great masters interpret to uplift and inspire to spiritual ecstasy. These rhythms make one forget body because they synchronize with body pulsations. For that reason they do not cause physical sensation.

Outer thinkers desire sensual rhythms which do not synchronize with body pulsations. Excitation can come to bodies only by changing the rhythm and tempo of their heartbeat. The moment the tempo of a heartbeat is slowed down in any musical rhythm, it slows down the heartbeat of the listener. That is why a baby goes to sleep when the mother croons a soothing lullaby. The power that music has within its rhythms and tempos to affect life, is inconceivable. The rhythms and tempos of the great world geniuses uplift the whole world toward its high heavens and causes those whom it can touch to seek the kingdom of heaven which centers them. Likewise, the discordant and split rhythms that are not in tune with Nature and the heartbeat of man multiply the sensations which the purely physical man seeks as entertainment for his body.

However, the one-two-three balanced rhythm of the waltz focuses attention upon the body by combining both the spiritual and physical emotions. The third beat, which characterizes the waltz, is in perfect balance with the two, and creates the desire for happy movement of balanced rhythms which combine the physical with the spiritual. Beyond that three in musical rhythms one cannot go without splitting one or all of them. The greater the departure from the balanced rhythms of Nature to the syncopated rhythms of man's desire for physical sensation, the greater the possibility of spiritual suppression in favor of physical degradation.

The power of music to degrade as well as to uplift is well exemplified in the jazz rhythms and tempos which shriek out their degrading power in raucous sounds that violate Nature's rhythms, as the sounds of a busy factory violate its peaceful countryside environment. Sensual men do not appreciate the music which deeply inspires inner thinking men. They have not sufficiently unfolded as yet to understand it. The power of spiritually inspired music is so great, however, that many thousands are gradually being transformed by oft repeated renditions.

Classical records are being distributed by the hundreds of thousands, and their effect is one of the most hopeful signs of the times, as well as being one of the greatest demonstrations of the power of music to transform sensual thinkers to spiritual thinkers. The greatest passion of every genius is to give to all the world treasures of heaven that have been given to him. A Beethoven, Mozart, Leonardo or Tennyson could not possibly withhold his treasures unto himself. Having become aware of their Oneness with their Creator, who gives freely of all He has, and without motive, they also must give freely and without motive.

The reward motive which is so characteristic of those who are sense-dominated, does not exist in Nature. Giving, in Nature, creates a vacuum that can be filled only by a balanced regiving. Giving, in Nature, is the first half of every electric cycle. It is an impossibility in Nature for one half of an electric cycle to remain uncompleted. It *must* complete itself. It cannot do otherwise. It must void itself by its own balancing counterpart. *No one can give, therefore, without a cosmic certainty of being equally regiven. For that reason the reward motive in Nature is not a part of God's plan.*

For the same reason it is very difficult for the genius to live in a material world. He *must* live, however. He must bargain with those who would buy from him. He must sell that which is his greatest happiness to give. It is against his very nature to be compelled to do that. It sickens his very Soul, for he is fully aware that he has been born ahead of his time and is compelled to live always in two worlds. His great recompense, however, is the fact that he can always escape from the outer world of material things and live in his own inner world of the spirit where he can commune with God to his heart's content and forget all things else, especially his body.

Judged by material standards the genius is an impractical dreamer, a subnormal who lacks the ability to make money as normal folks do. As children they are usually low in their marks, for the educational plan of this age stultifies genius by "educating" the brain instead of unfolding the Mind. Thomas Edison was sent home from school with a note from the teacher advising his mother to put him in a school for subnormals. The practice of schools has been to develop a civilization which has learned to *remember and repeat* instead of unfolding their imaginative faculties by teaching them to *think and know.*

The intelligence test for high scholarship marks is based upon how many questions one can answer. To attain great heights in that respect one has to have a photographic memory which outward-sensed thinkers readily develop. It is impossible, however, for anyone to have a photographic Mind. That is why a genius is often considered stupid in school. A great many children are utterly ruined by this process. They may really be the brightest children in the school with strong creative abilities that a few years of suppression of their creative faculties ruin for world purposes.

Information is not knowledge. It is of no importance whatsoever that one should remember the date of Caesar's death or the date of the Battle of Waterloo. One might be able to answer every question in the encyclopedia and yet have no knowledge. A student who received a low intelligence rating because he could not remember the name of the river which flowed into the Caspian Sea, and the capital of Finland, might be consoled by the probability that Shakespeare or Dickens might also not be able to answer these questions. Under such a memory system the boys who have the greatest initiative, imagination and resourcefulness could be judged the most stupid, while the plodder with a photographic memory and no initiative could be judged the brightest.

Information might be likened to food which will nourish a body when it has been digested and enters the blood stream. Information can lead to knowledge when digested through reasoning and Mind-thinking, but as long as it is only brain-recording it is of no value to creative expression. To remember and repeat, through experimentation, reasoning and assembling other brain recordings of observed effects, does not constitute knowledge. It but indicates cleverness. This highly technical world of many skills is very much more the result of great cleverness in the assembling of observed effects of motion than it is the result of knowledge.

When the world begins to acquire knowledge it will show the effects of it in human relations instead of chemical and metallurgical relations. The human race has not

yet acquired sufficient knowledge to know the law which
makes it possible for man to live with man—or to know
the relation of woman to man. It is too concerned with
the application of the many physical laws to the relation
of physical matter to give thought to God's one and only
law that governs spiritual relations.

World desire for knowing what holds the atom together
has only an economical and material basis. Such knowledge "would be worth untold millions" in new machines
and comforts for man. That is the basis of world desire
for knowledge. It has only a money value. Its spiritual
value has not yet entered into human consciousness. For
that very reason God will not let man have that knowledge, and man will never find it while he seeks in the
wrong direction. Actually the answer is right before
man's eyes but he does not recognize it while his eyes have
outer vision alone. When inner vision comes through inner thinking he will then recognize it in all its simplicity.
All who have arrived at the Cosmic Mind state know what
holds the atom together, and they do not need cyclotrons
to tell them that secret of the invisible universe. *Knowledge of CAUSE can never be acquired from motion. It
can be acquired only from the Source of motion.*

"Empirical knowledge" is a term used as a name for
the results of sensed observation. Knowledge cannot be
gained through the senses, for the senses are unable to
see the true picture of any effect of motion whatsoever.
No effect in Nature is what it seems to be. A three-
dimensional objective universe is as much of an illusion as
a cinema is an illusion. Truth and reality cannot be de-
duced from a simulation of truth and reality. This universe of motion is but a cosmic cinema projected upon the
screen of space from its light Source in thinking Mind.
Its reality is at its Source, and not in the projected image.

The most imaginative years of life are between the ages of three and fourteen. During those years whatever is creative in a child should be developed and encouraged. Instead of "cramming" for examinations, where questions are to be asked, children should be encouraged to take an hour's walk, either in the woods, or through a store, or around a city block, then asked to write an essay on what they saw, or what their thoughts were. A creative education should be based upon doing things which cause the children to *think and know,* rather than to *remember and repeat.* During school years the main object should be to develop creative expression by stimulating the imagination. That is helpful in awakening that spark of genius which is in everyone, for creative expression compels inner thinking. A small percentage of time should be spent in giving them the essentials for that expression, such as simple mathematics, grammar, spelling and geography. Every other study, such as history or languages, one should get by reading during subsequent years.

It would be better for the new generation if all history study could be withdrawn from the schools. It is all written upon a war basis and the glorification of the desire in pagan man to kill his fellow man. History, as written for schools, is a war to war inventory. Its motive is to promote hero worship of world-killers. The motive upon which history should be written, if its purpose is to enlighten the human race instead of degrading it, is to teach the lessons of agony that wars have given to man. They should be lessons which demonstrate that war does not pay, as some of our crime lessons demonstrate that crime does not pay.

We had a long period of crime movies which promoted and increased crime and juvenile delinquency because it glorified the criminal. Burglars, killers and outlaws were characterized as heroes. The effect upon the world's increase in crime and youth delinquency was so noticeable that the entire motive had to be changed to act as a lesson for crime determent. All history study should be rewritten upon this basis.

Drawing, painting, sculpture and music should be a part of every child's education. Children always love to draw. Desire for drawing and painting develops in early childhood. It should be encouraged in every way. Likewise, the music of the great masters should not only be heard, but analyzed until thoroughly understood in comparison with the split rhythms of sensualism.

The principle of "educating" the senses, instead of unfolding the treasures of the Mind in creative expression, is not only very hurtful to the individual but is hurtful to the effort of keeping the Christian spirit alive, and multiplying it throughout the land. Every accentuation of sensuous thinking lessens the desire for spiritual expression and increases all of the qualities which the human race must eliminate in order to progress towards its goal. To spend valuable years in thus stultifying and smothering that spark of divinity, which must some day be illumined into activity for every man, is a great and tragic pity.

My husband, who has achieved masterliness in all of the five fine arts, besides making invaluable contributions to science, often says that the most fortunate happening of his life was being taken out of school at nine. He fully knew his destiny at seven years of age, as practically all geniuses do.

SUMMARY

Jesus said: "Seek ye the kingdom of heaven within you." The genius has come very close to having reached that center which Jesus had, Himself, completely found.

When this stage in human unfolding has been reached by enough of the human race to dominate its transactions, one with another, wars will be impossible. Material values are the basis of all wars. The genius stage of unfolding places no value whatsoever upon material things. Greed and acquisitiveness is not in it. The sense of evil is not in it. It would be impossible and unthinkable for a Beethoven or Sibelius to even think the inharmonies which are necessary to wage war.

The only way to hold a civilization together is to bring a cosmic harmony into it through transactions based upon love. It is impossible to hold it together as a workable organization in any other way. We have now reached the point in this man-made world where hate, suspicion and greed are sitting at conference tables to bargain with each other. The more they bargain the greater the necessity for increased armament.

Those who sit at the bargaining tables are men the conquerors, and fathers of conquerors. Women, the mothers and peacemakers, are not with their men at the conference tables. There will never be peace on earth and good will toward man, until fatherhood and motherhood sit together as world-fatherhood and motherhood to extend loving service to one another. Such unbalance is a violation of God's one inviolate law which no earthly power can set aside and survive, as man is now so futilely trying to do. Perhaps it is that woman is the only hope of saving this civilization!

CHAPTER VI

Cosmic Consciousness

The fourth stage of human unfoldment, of sensual man to spiritual man, is the high stage of Cosmic Consciousness. This stage is as far ahead of the genius stage as the genius is ahead of the barbarian. It is difficult for those who have not yet reached the genius stage to comprehend that stage, but it is possible for everyone to recognize that it is existent because the works of the great Cosmic geniuses are evident everywhere. Everyone knows that there really are superhuman people like Michelangelo, Brahms or Mozart even though they know that they, themselves, are not like them. Likewise, there have been about a hundred great geniuses whose works are so conspicuously in evidence that there is no question that a much higher state of mentality is possible than the average mentality.

The state of Cosmic Consciousness was first referred to in India as "The Brahmic Bliss." It was also referred to as "Nirvana," meaning the ultimate goal of mankind in which all identity is lost in the universal Identity. The New Testament referred to it as being "in the Spirit" and as "the Anointing." It is also referred to as "the state of ecstasy." Cosmic Consciousness is so rare, however, that there have probably not been more than fifteen completely illumined examples in all history. By that I mean those who have had the experience of complete severance of sensation from Consciousness, followed by long periods, rather than those who had but momentary flashes and found themselves in a state of some confusion.

Dr. Richard Maurice Bucke [1] is the greatest authority upon Cosmic Consciousness. His own personal illumination lasted but a few seconds but so completely transformed him that he devoted the rest of his life to the study of other cases, and in writing a book which is of inestimable value to those who are seeking to awaken their own spiritual awareness. The symptoms he describes will enable one to recognize those symptoms of awakening genius or Cosmic Consciousness, which they may have experienced but do not comprehend. Dr. Bucke lists about forty cases, and erringly includes Jesus among these. Jesus is the only one who has ever reached the highest stage of divine awareness, Christ Consciousness, which will be described next.

Cosmic Consciousness utterly transforms those who have already reached the high stage of the genius into an incredible greater stage of spiritual Mind-existence. Some of these cases have actually bridged the genius stage, or passed through it, without knowing it. When Cosmic Consciousness consumes one with its illumination of Soul-Mind, it comes very suddenly, without any warning whatsoever, and without being suspected. There are no indications of it, nor can it be induced by anybody, no matter how familiar one becomes with its reality.

Full and sudden Cosmic illumination is attended with a flash of Cosmic Light which is invisible to everyone except the recipient of it. The New Testament describes Paul's spiritual illumination into Cosmic Consciousness:

[1] Cosmic Consciousness, by Dr. Richard Maurice Bucke. E. P. Dutton Company, New York. Quotations from this book will appear in this chapter and be indicated by an asterisk.

"He became as one transformed." He was transformed because from that moment he was as different a mentality as the mentality of a full-grown man exceeds the mentality of a child.

What happens is that the doors to "the kingdom of heaven" seem to open suddenly, and all the glory of God's Light of all-knowledge and all-power become revealed. The recipient becomes transformed with knowledge of his absolute unity with God. He at once begins to think with God and know His thoughts as being his own. He suddenly becomes fully aware that the Voice which he first heard millions of years ago as instinct, then as intuition, then as inspiration, is God's Voice and his own, as ONE. There is no longer any mystery about it, no vagueness, no yearning to pierce the impenetrable. He *has* pierced it. He *has* found that center of stillness which his Soul is. He can now knowingly say: I and my Father are ONE, for he has become that One. This is what is meant by revelations. It is knowledge which has been cosmically revealed.

The explanation of the flash of light which accompanies all cases of complete Cosmic Consciousness, is caused by a short circuit that severs the two centers of sensation in the two lobes of the brain from the seat of Consciousness. Such a flash occurs also at the instant of death. It has been photographed many times.

One distinctive feature of Cosmic Consciousness is that everyone who experiences it states the same things. They all experience a tremendous state of ecstasy, which is the God Nature—a deep conviction of Love and the Oneness of God and man—and the idea of evil and death entirely disappears into their complete knowledge of immortality and eternal life. Whatever a Cosmic Conscious mystic writes is fully understood by any other mystic. No matter how different the words may be, their sense is universal. Their language is alike but it is strange to all but those of high culture or great spiritual unfolding.

For better understanding of these divine ones among men I will quote characteristic sayings of the eight most highly illumined ones. The first known case is the writer of the Bhaga Vad Gita. No one knows who he was but his immortal words have already outlived thousands of years and will endure as long as man endures. The following quotations sing their own glory in the unmistakable language of the divine mystic:

"Another Sun gleams there; another Moon;
Another Light,—not Dusk, nor Dawn, nor Noon—
Which they who once behold return no more;
They have attained My rest, life's utmost boon." (Chap. XV)

* * *

"Fain would I see, as thou Thyself declar'st it, Sovereign Lord, the likeness of Thy Form wholly revealed. O Thou Divinest One, if this can be, if I may bear the sight, make Thyself visible, Lord of all prayers. Show me Thy very self, Eternal God.

"Behold! this is the Universe!—Look! what is live and dead I gather all in one in Me! Gaze, as thy lips have said, on God ETERNAL, VERY GOD! See Me! see what thou prayest.

"Thou can'st not!—nor with human eyes ever mayest! Therefore I give thee sense divine. Have other eyes, new light! And look, this is My glory, unveiled to mortal sight." (Chap. XI)

* * *

"Of many thousand mortals, one, perchance,
Striveth for Truth; and of these few that strive—
Nay, and rise high,—one only—here and there—
Knoweth Me as I am, the very Truth." (Chap. VII)

* * *

"For in this world Being is twofold; the Divided, one;
The Undivided, one. All things that live
Are 'the Divided.' That which sits apart,
'The Undivided.' " (Chap. XV)

* * *

Gautama, known as The Buddha, was the second
known case of Cosmic Consciousness. He lived about five
hundred years before Jesus came, and his life has affected
the Orient as deeply as the life of Jesus affected the Oc-
cident. He was the son of a very rich landowner and lived
in great luxury at the time the "supernatural light" descended upon him. He left all this, and his wife and son,
to live alone in the wilderness for a long time. He then
began to teach men to seek eternal peace within themselves through much meditation, aloneness and complete
renunciation of worldly matters.

Like all who are illumined, The Buddha gained all his
real knowledge from within himself. He decried the kind
of so-called knowledge of the schools as superficial, if not
useless. This point is well illustrated in his story of a
youth who returned from school with much ego after
twelve years of classical studies: "The boy's father said to
him, * Svetaketu, as you are so conceited, considering
yourself so well read, and so stern, my dear, have you
ever asked for that instruction by which we hear that
which cannot be heard, by which we perceive that which
cannot be perceived, by which we know that which cannot
be known?"

This quotation is proof that The Buddha passed
through the genius stage without having known it, or if
he did know it, no historian has ever understood that fact
sufficiently to record it. Perhaps the essence of his experience is in the following words: * "That one (the self),

though never stirring, is swifter than thought. The senses never reached it, it walked before them. Though standing still, it overtakes the others who are running. The moving spirit bestows powers upon it. It stirs and it stirs not. It is far and likewise near. It is inside of all this and it is outside of all this.

"And he who beholds all beings in the self and the self in all beings, he never turns away from it. When to a man who understands, the self has become all things, what sorrow, what trouble can there be to him who once beheld that unity?"

When the teachings of all mystics are thoroughly comprehended there could be but one religion, for the teachings are one. There can be no fault in any religion which seeks to know God. The fault lies only in the inability of man to *see* God, *know* God and *be* God. The human race must unfold in orderly stages. Comprehension will come to all men, but *man himself can hasten it by deeply desiring it, and by deeply seeking within himself for it through much meditation and wordless prayer.*

Plotinus and Mohammed were born into the world during the twelve centuries of Dark Ages. It is more than probable that Dante also was Illuminate. It is claimed that he was, but I am not sufficiently convinced of that fact to include him.

Plotinus was born in A.D. 204 and lived seventy years. He discarded all that is called scholarship, meaning that so-called knowledge which the senses record upon human brains as memory impressions. It is important that the present generations of men should understand his exalted point of view, for the modern system of creating scholars is the superficial one of accumulating information concerning effects of motion, upon the assumption that such information is knowledge. In that sense we have no scholars which have been school-made. If we have scholars they are Self-made. Plotinus uses the word "appearances" in the sense which we use the word "information." I quote him:

* "External objects present us only with appearances. Concerning them, therefore, we may be said to possess *opinion* rather than *knowledge*.

"Our question lies with the ideal reality that exists behind appearance. How does the Mind perceive these ideals? Are they without us, and is the reason, like sensation, occupied with objects external to itself?

"What certainty would we then have—what assurance that our perception was infallible? The object perceived would be a something different from the mind perceiving it. We should have then an image instead of reality.

"It would be monstrous to believe for a moment that the mind was unable to perceive ideal truth exactly as it is, and that we had not certainty and real knowledge concerning the world of intelligence.

"It follows, therefore, that this region of truth is not to be investigated as a thing *external to us,* and so imperfectly known. *It is within us.* Here the objects we contemplate and that which contemplates are identical—both are thought.

"The subject cannot surely know an object different from itself. It is the agreement of the mind with itself.

"Consciousness, therefore, is the sole basis of certainty. The mind is its own witness. Reason sees in itself that which is above itself as its source; and again that which is below itself is still itself once more."

How very different is this language to that which is familiar to our schools and scholars who applaud the brilliance of the student who can remember and repeat more events and incidents than another student. Observe also that Plotinus told man to seek Truth within him, as Jesus did.

Consider the knowledge of Plotinus herein expressed. He is asked: "How can we know the Infinite?"

* "I answer, not by reason. It is the office of reason to distinguish and define. The Infinite, therefore, cannot be ranked among its objects. You can only apprehend the Infinite by a faculty superior to reason, by entering into a state in which you are your finite self no longer—in which the divine essence is communicated to you. This is ecstasy (Cosmic Consciousness). It is the liberation of your mind from its finite consciousness."

Mohammed is one of the great Illumined. Three great religions grew out of the words of three great mystics. The religions are all different but the words and teachings are the same. Moslemism is in practice totally different from either Christianity or Buddhism, but that is the fault of its practice, not of its principle. This could also be said about Christianity and Buddhism.

Those who would compare the teachings of Mohammed, Jesus and The Buddha would find not one whit of difference in essence, also if the words of all these three are compared with those of Francis Bacon (Shakespeare), Walt Whitman, Jacob Behmen, Balzac or John Yepes, they would all be the same in essence, even though the words differ. Mohammed used the word "Paradise" in the same sense that Jesus used the words "Kingdom of God," and The Buddha used the word "Nirvana." Mohammed said: * "This is the day of eternity. Enter into it in peace," which parallels the words of Jesus: "The kingdom of God is within you." John Yepes said: * "God is always in man,

and very commonly the soul is aware of His presence.
It is as if he slept in the soul. If he wakes up only once in
a man's whole life the experience of that moment affects
the whole life."

Another modern mystic who has transformed millions
of lives and turned their eyes to the Light is Bahá'u'lláh,
the founder of a great religious movement known as the
Bahá'í Faith, although he was not listed in Dr. Bucke's
classic work as an Illuminate.

The unfolding of physical man to spiritual man always
comes through the revelations of Cosmic Messengers who
have been illumined with higher knowledge by becoming
wholly Mind for even a brief period, but always enough
to transform the world through their own transformation.
A study of the ascent of man will reveal that each upward
step has been caused by the advent of a Cosmic Messenger who periodically appears among men with new
knowledge which has been revealed to him for that purpose. It will also reveal the fact that when any man of
higher knowledge and ideals than the average of his day
comes into the world he is persecuted, ridiculed, imprisoned, tortured and even crucified by the uncompre-
hending multitudes. The greater the message and Messenger, the greater the torture. These Messengers who
transform the world with new knowledge always meet
with great personal suffering for their priceless gifts. The
inventor, the pioneers in new ways and methods, the
genius in the fine arts or any man who dares to depart
from traditional thinking, always meet with ridicule in
various measures and forms until the value of his gift to
the world is recognized.

Jesus died on the cross. Leonardo died in poverty.
Galileo was tortured. Copernicus was spurned and ridi-

culed. Bacon was forced to hide his identity in Shakespeare. Spinoza constantly feared arrest. Whitman was despised and his books banned. Mozart, Liszt, Chopin and Schumann were hireling entertainers for the rich. Even Goodyear, in our day, suffered untold agonies for his gift of vulcanized rubber which revolutionized transportation. The many always oppress the few. It is difficult for Love and for knowledge to come into the world. Crucifixion always awaits Love. Knowledge is always launched upon the sea of ignorance. That is why the journey of man is so long, so hard, and so slow.

In Bahá'u'lláh is an exemplification of this trait of human nature, for he was tortured and imprisoned in chains for years in a filthy black dungeon, with thieves and murderers, until he was near death. Many of his followers were imprisoned with him and executed, yet the cosmic ecstasy of an eternally happy man remained with him through his far greater sufferings than even a crucifixion.

Bahá'u'lláh's writings and teachings are the same in essence as those of all other Illuminati. They vary only in their wording, but not in their meaning. Where Jesus uses the word "within," Bahá'u'lláh uses the word "insight." Both have the same meaning, however. In describing the revelations of mystics he said: "Without words we speak, we communicate, we converse with God and hear the answer."

It is universal in all mystics to as frankly say they talk with God as it is for one man to say he talked with another. No greater evidence of Bahá'u'lláh's great understanding of the God-presence in man could be found than the following extract from his teachings: "It is said that Moses in the wilderness heard the voice of God. But that wilderness, that holy land was his own heart. All of us, when we attain to a true spiritual condition, can hear the voice of God speaking to us in that wilderness."

Bahá'u'lláh thoroughly comprehended the permanently ecstatic state of God's Mind to such an extent that nothing could affect his own eternal state of happiness and the contemplation of beauty and harmony which exists in all of God's Creation. Even while suffering great agony of body in prison he refused to deviate from the principle which he taught, to the effect that nothing ill could happen to a man if he is happy. Take note of the fact that he said that while undergoing great physical suffering.

He said: "Afflictions and troubles are due to the state of not being content with what God has ordained for you. If one submits himself to God he is happy." By this he means that whatever may be your destiny while working with God, that you must submit to, for that is your Glory.

When asked where happiness comes from he answered: "Because all existing things move according to my wish; therefore I do not do anything contrary to my desire; thus I have no sorrow.

"There is no doubt that all beings move by the will of God, and I have given up my own will, desiring the will of God. Thus my will becomes the will of God, for there is nothing of myself. All are moving by his will, yet they are moving by my will. In this case I am very happy."

The purity, the friendliness and happiness of his teachings cannot but ennoble anyone who tries to fathom their depths. The Bahá'í Faith which he founded is without doctrine and completely tolerant of all religions and faiths, and expresses the desire for that day of unity when there will be but one religion. In all his teachings tolerance for things which men do and say is conspicuous. His attitude is that man does not know what he is doing when he does evil things, for he is but on his way to knowing. That is the same attitude expressed by Jesus when He said: "Father, forgive them, for they know not what they do."

He condemned nobody, even while expressing his regret that others teach, or practice, anything which was contrary to God's law, as he so plainly did in admonishing St. Paul for his disapproval of marriage and for prophesying that sects would arise which would be celibate. Bahá'-u'lláh laid this fault down to superstition and ignorance of God's law.

His tolerance extended to even his prophecies about the coming of other Messengers who would come with new knowledge suited to their day and age, and specifically foretold of a scientific revelation.

The Bahá'í Faith is world-wide and its followers give evidence of the inspiring nature of its teachings by their exemplary lives and actions.

All who have reached the Cosmic Conscious stage have attained full God-awareness. They not only know God, but they unhesitatingly state their Oneness with Him. Jesus not only said: "I and My Father are One," but said that every man is One with Him and with God when he knows that he is. All Cosmic messengers have said that same thing, in essence if not in the same words. The only difference between any man and Jesus, or The Buddha, or Shakespeare, or Paderewski, is divine awareness. Nothing else. Every Cosmic Conscious messenger very plainly tells you that, but few believe it because few comprehend it. Long ages of outward thinking have unfitted them for comprehending it. A very few years of inward, meditative thinking will give one greater God-awareness than centuries of outward thinking.

For another example of the similarity of Cosmic thinkers, compare these words of Jacob Behmen: * "Spiritual knowledge cannot be communicated from one intellect to another, but must be sought for in the spirit of God" —with Walt Whitman who says: * "Wisdom is of the soul; it cannot be passed from one having it to another not having it." Behman also wrote: * "The gate was opened to me that in one quarter of an hour I saw and knew more than if I had been many years together at a university, . . ."

All of them are in full agreement that those who are illumined into Cosmic Consciousness are given a profound wisdom—or knowledge—of the very essence of God which can never be acquired from books, or schools, or any outside source whatsoever. Likewise, all Cosmic Mystics have said in essence: "God is Love—and I am Love," and that all men are one brotherhood and also: "I am all men." Walt Whitman, Francis Bacon (Shakespeare) and Mary Baker Eddy, are the three greatest mystics of the late centuries. Their works are fairly saturated with the idea of love, unity, brotherhood of man and spiritual identity.

Whitman says: * "And I know that the hand of God is the elder hand of my own, And I know that the spirit of God is the eldest brother of my own. And that all men ever born are also my brothers, and the women my sisters and lovers, And that a kelson [2] of creation is love."

In describing the "supernatural" flash of light which always accompanies full illumination, Whitman says:

[2] Kelson, or keelson, is the foundation upon which a ship is built.

* "As in a swoon, one instant,
    Another sun, ineffable full-dazzles me,
    And all the orbs I knew, and brighter, unknown orbs;
    One instant of the future land, Heaven's land."

How much these words are like those in the Bhaga Vad
Gita, written thousands of years ago!

No words could more forcibly express the emptiness of
the world of material values which seems to be the first
aim of those who have made this world what it is, than
these of Whitman:

* "Hast never come to thee an hour,
    A sudden gleam divine, precipitating, bursting
    all these bubbles, fashions wealth?
    These eager business aims—books, politics,
    arts, armours,
    To utter nothingness."

Mary Baker Eddy was the only woman who has been
known to have reached that spiritual stage of Cosmic
Consciousness. With Walt Whitman, she was the most
recent. Her name was not included in Dr. Bucke's list
of Immortals who had arrived at the stage of Cosmic
Consciousness, but it should have been. Mrs. Eddy experienced her first Cosmic illumination when she was
twelve years old. She did not know what it meant at that
time. No one who has that experience ever does at the
time it happens, for it is so rare that few know about it,
also it is entirely unanticipated. She describes it as follows: "and a soft glow of ineffable joy came over me."
She was in a fever at the time and the fever suddenly disappeared. That is also characteristic of the transformation
which takes place during an illumination. She also said
that "other incidents of an extraordinary nature" oc-

curred at the time. This same experience of Cosmic illumination again occurred when she was forty-five. She
was seriously ill at the time, but again she was restored
to normalcy during that short period of ecstasy which always accompanies the illumination.

As in all other cases of Cosmic Consciousness she was
given the knowledge that all Mind is one, which she calls
"divine Mind,—that the body is not the person—that
there is no life, truth or intelligence in matter—and that
there is no *evil* nor death in Nature." Such revelations
coming under such conditions are full and complete evidence of her Cosmic illumination. Further evidence of
it lies in the words and manner of her teachings which
she imparted to others.

She very clearly denied that sin existed in Nature and
explained it as a belief in man's mortal mind—meaning
the senses. She also taught what all Cosmic Illuminates
know, that Jesus came to save mankind from a *belief* in
sin, and not that He came to save man from sin. She called
world attention to the fact that Jesus never used the word
"sin" with the connotation of evil which men give to it.
Jesus used the word in the sense of experience, as He used
it in the case of the man with the palsy, to whom He said:
"Son, be of good cheer, thy sins be forgiven thee."

Mrs. Eddy also firmly states that God, the Creator,
created only that which was good—and that truth and
goodness are one—therefore nothing real could be existent which is not good—and manifests truth in Him.
Nothing is more convincing evidence of her right to be
included in the very immortals who have been illumined
with the Light of God's Mind than the following extracts
from her teachings: "Man is not a material habitation of
the Soul: he is himself spiritual.—Man is idea, the image

of love: He is not physique. . . . Man is the reflection of God, or Mind, and therefore is eternal: that which has no separate mind from God; that which has not a single quality underived from Deity; that which possesses no life, intelligence nor creative power of his own, but reflects spiritually all that belongs to his Maker. . . . Man is incapable of sin, sickness, and death."

Such Cosmic knowledge does not come from earthly teachings. They are not in any of man's books, nor were they taught to her by the church which she attended. Cosmic knowledge comes to earth only through divine messengers who have known the Oneness with the One Mind of this universe. Such knowledge comes only to one in billions of humans. Mary Baker Eddy may never have heard of Cosmic Consciousness, so rare it is, but she frankly declared that: "I won my way to absolute conclusions through divine revelations, reason and demonstration." That is what Cosmic Consciousness is.

My husband's entire scientific knowledge came that way. In May of 1921 he had no knowledge whatsoever of astronomy, chemistry, mathematics, electricity nor the construction of matter. He did not care to know them for his desires were in the fine arts.

In one timeless flash he became master of all the sciences and knew as much in that one flash as he knows now. In 1926 he gave his first gift to the scientific world in The Russell Charts of the Elements which completed the incomplete and incorrect Mendeléef Charts. In this first of many contributions, he charted and announced the existence of urium and uridium, and the four other transuranium elements which made atomic fission possible, also deuterium and tritrium and the other four hydrogen isotopes, which made the H-bomb and heavy water

possible. The world does not know urium and uridium
by these names, however, for many years later when science verified their existence they renamed these two elements plutonium and neptunium.

His contributions since then have been many but the
cosmogony which God gave him is so unlike the tradi-
tionally accepted one that it may be many years before its
value may be recognized.

All that I have ever known was revealed to me cosmically in the same manner. I also did not receive the formal
education of the schools. That is why our combined
knowledge, forcibly presented, may enlighten enough of
those who are ready for it, to save the world in this
eleventh hour of its danger. Neither my husband's knowledge nor mine ever came from books or schools, however.
It was cosmically inspired. Knowledge has never come
into the world in any other way.

Circumstances forced me into a great aloneness in my
youth and these were my rich years, my formative years,
which finally culminated in my own illumining in two
great periods. These two periods so utterly transformed
me that a greater power of Self-expression came to me
than I had ever known. I found that *whatever* I desired to
do I *could* do. And that is what you would find if you
sought within your Self for knowledge and power as we
have.

It is important that I tell you some of the facts regarding the way we received all of our knowledge in order that
you may acquire cosmic knowledge if you so desire. All
Illuminates will tell you the same thing. Down through
the ages they have said that all knowledge could be obtained *only* from within—that the kingdom of heaven
was within—that all else will be added unto him who

seeks it from within. The whole purpose of this book is to point the way to all knowledge and power for *you*. To attain it you have to acquire the power to *think inwardly* instead of to *sense outwardly*.

Begin early in life to do that. Do not wait until tradition and materialism insulates your Soul by building a wall around it. That is why I felt impelled to break away from the treadmill of tradition in my childhood. I was as certain of my destiny and purpose at three years of age as I am now. My education came from looking into the hearts of the people of all the world and of Nature. It was my good fortune to be able to travel extensively in Asia and Africa as well as the English-speaking continents. I made a great discovery in so doing, which will be helpful to you if you apply it. I found that greater knowing comes from the silences of what people do not say than from what they do say. It is that way in Nature. The silences reach the Soul with their deep meanings while sounds must be translated from sensed awareness to Mind intelligence. The silent words from the hearts of all men told me that all mankind is essentially GOOD. All are seeking happiness and love. There is no evil in the search for love, so there can be no evil in a balanced universe which is all GOOD.

Our present-day world is not conducive to the search for love. Its human relations are based upon outer sensing. When they are based upon inner thinking our human relations basis *must* change, for mankind will then have learned that what he does to others he is doing to himself.

A new language with its own meaning has come into the world from its illumined ones. The genius can hear Nature's rhythms with his inner ears, and see its spectrum harmonies with inner eyes, but the Cosmic being can clearly comprehend the construction of matter and the workings of electric polarization as it divides and multiplies gravity into the contracted matter of suns and divides it to create space. In less time than it takes to write this description, one who knows nothing of the universe, knows all of it. In that brief flash he becomes master chemist and knows the stars of heaven beyond all men. The explanation of this fact is simple. When man's Mind and God's become one, their thinking is one. They do not become synchronized as two but *are* one. That which heretofore seemed to pulse within them separately, pulses universally. The Illuminate suddenly becomes "in tune with the Infinite." He instantly becomes the Thinker and Knower instead of being an extension of the Thinker and Knower.

God's Mind thinks in octave thought-waves. Every creative thought is electrically divided into octave thought-waves which require four efforts to create matter into living bodies and four more efforts to void those bodies. Every action and reaction in Nature repeats this simple life-death principle. There is no exception to it throughout the universe. Every incoming-outgoing breath repeats it, every sound repeats it, and the pulsing of the stars repeats it. Within that simple principle lies all knowledge, for in it is all CAUSE which can be known, and all effect which can be comprehended. Its simplicity is instantly recognized by the highly spiritual inward thinker who is enabled to strip it of its complexity by making it stand still and be only one, instead of many billions in one second.

To the Cosmic Thinker who can make the universe stand still and void time, Creation unfolds from the Soul of idea to create form. All forms are thought-forms which appear, disappear and reappear forever. When one sees forms unfold from seed, and refold into seed, one sees all there is to see and to know. There is nothing else to know, for Mind is the seed of Creation from which all forms unfold from zero of invisibility to become visible for a time, before refolding into invisible Mind.

That is all there is to all philosophy, all sciences and all mathematics. Certain great Illuminati, whom no one has ever known, left messages in great stone pyramids for future man to decipher, and to tell them of their existence, long ages ago. These illumined ones knew astronomy and mathematics beyond perhaps even our day. They could not have acquired this knowledge from books for there were no books or universities. The measurements of these pyramids prove that they not only could measure the diameter of the earth, with great precision, but a hundred other astronomical and mathematical measurements proved vast knowledge in other directions. They gave strong evidence of possessing an extrasensory perception, such as our civilization has not yet attained.

In one of these pyramids events three thousand years ahead are accurately foretold. Knowing Cause these ancient mystics could deduce the effects which must follow. These few must have founded some brotherhood through which they kept their knowledge alive, for the same principles and measurements are repeated in part in Tibet and the civilizations which lie buried one upon another in the Andes and Central America.

CONCLUSION

These men of great knowledge acquired their knowledge from somewhere other than universities and books, for there were neither universities nor books in their day.

According to modern educational standards all their vast knowledge would be denied them and considered of no avail because it was not acquired through the legitimate channels, which means through the *senses.*

Today's intellectual world denies that knowledge can be spiritually acquired through revelation and inspiration, which means by talking to God. The lesson mankind should learn, through the lives of the greatest men who have ever lived on this planet, is that knowledge can *only* be acquired through the inner spirit of man and not through his body, or through matter, or through motion. Knowledge comes from *within,* not from without. The men who have been the world's most priceless treasures probably never attended school, or if they did they were not counted as the most brilliant students.

Whether or not such men as Bacon, Buddha, Beethoven, Leonardo, Jesus, Tennyson or Schumann ever attended school, it is most certain that the great knowledge these divine messengers gave to the world was not a part of any school curriculum. Their knowledge came from the spiritual fountains of themselves. They had found the kingdom of heaven and all that heaven had to give was "added unto them."

The great lesson for each man to learn from the lives and works of these immortals is that each man's own immortality can be found only by inner thinking, and deep meditation, and deep, wordless spiritual prayer from the heart, and not from the lips. The only way the Silent Voice can become audible to man is through inner ears. The only way man can vision God is through inner eyes. That is the only way man can knowingly work with God and God with man to produce enduring things. It is the only way that God, the Creator, can be manifested in Man, the Creator.

Likewise, the only way there can be a spiritual birth in the world is through spiritual thinking which establishes values based upon man rather than matter. The greatest motive for world-crime lies in greed to obtain money. For this he sells his Soul by crucifying love and human values. When man learns that man is man's greatest asset he will serve his fellowman instead of killing him as he does now for material values. Crime will disappear when the motive for crime disappears, and peace will come when *love* appears.

CHAPTER VII

Christ Consciousness

The fifth and final stage of spiritual unfoldment is Christ Consciousness. It is the highest stage of human attainment which all mankind will eventually reach.

Jesus of Nazareth is the only man in all recorded history who has ever reached that stage of complete God-awareness. He was so fully illumined with the Light, and the Love which God is, and the omniscience and omnipotence which God is, that he could knowingly say: "I and My Father are ONE."

The birth and life of Jesus was the supreme event of all history. The life of God's Messenger of Love has been a Light which will illumine the world forever, and His death by man's hands plunged man's world into the dark for twelve long cruel centuries.

He who has finally attained the Cosmic Light in full awareness has passed beyond fear of death, for he knows there is no death in eternal life.

He who has reached that Source of eternal Good knows there can be no evil in God's balanced universe.

He whose thinking has been as one unit of Creation has now become the universal Thinker with the One Mind Source of all that has ever been or ever will be.

He who has been subject to effect in matter becomes Cause. He has learned to command matter by ages of learning to obey its commands. He can dissolve and void the illnesses of man by projecting His balance into the unbalanced condition which caused them.

Having become universal in His thinking He is aware of any thoughts anywhere. All man's thoughts are known to Him through the universality of the One Mind whom He is.

Jesus was the greatest Intelligence the world has ever known. He gave to the world the greatest teachings it has ever known. Extrasensory perception, which is just beginning to manifest in the telepathic and clairvoyant stage of man, was full and complete in Jesus.

That inconceivably wonderful illumination into Christ Consciousness exalted Jesus to the God state of Universal Oneness. It was thenceforth impossible for Him to see any man as being separate and apart from Himself and from other men. Jesus knew of the electrical unity of everything in all the universe. He not only *knew* it with His Mind but could *see* it with his extrasensory vision. The aura which connects every object in the universe with every other object was perfectly visible to Him. Because of His unlimited knowledge and power He was enabled to do many things which were so far beyond the comprehension of man that they were explainable only to man as being supernatural or miraculous.

The time will come when you will be able to command matter to obey you as He was enabled to do. When that time comes in your knowing the world will then know the naturalness of that which now seems so supernatural. As man unfolds into full mental growth it is beyond his powers to either see or comprehend any state of Mind which he, himself, has not yet experienced.

When we observe that people of today do not even understand the much lower stage of genius, how very much more difficult it is, and has been, for man to comprehend the divine state when they find it in flesh and blood like their own. How often we hear people say that geniuses are especially born and that they can never be like them because of that fact. People do not deny the existence of geniuses, however, for their extraordinary mental power is too evident in their works for denial.

Neither can Jesus be denied, for He too is known by His works, but He cannot be comprehended because Christ Consciousness is too far beyond the present stage of Mind-unfolding for comprehension to be possible. It is more upon the order of man's thinking to place Him in the realms of the supernatural.

It is sufficient for everyone in the world to know that Christ Consciousness is the ultimate goal for every man. It should be a glorious thought and the strongest possible incentive for right thinking and acting in this life in order to be a little farther ahead in each repetition of our unfolding.

The only purpose of man on earth is to manifest God. Long aeons pass during which time man manifests his physical self instead of his spiritual divinity, but the aeons pass, and man learns his lesson eventually.

Your journey is for the purpose of making that transition from the physical dark to the spiritual Light of Illumined Mind. That is what Creation is for. God is Love. You are given your life by your Creator to learn how to express Love until you become Love.

The world of man has hardly unfolded far enough to even know what Love means. The aeons will tell it to him. His own joys and agonies will tell it to him, until some day he will know.

Peace will then come to him, with all the happiness,

beauty and romance that Love is as he passes through one uplifting stage after another to become the genius, the Cosmic Knower and the supremely exalted Christ Conscious Being. The journey of the individual will then end in the ultimate Oneness of God and man.

PART II

*"In vain we build the city
if we do not first build the man."*

Edwin Markham

CHAPTER VIII

Universal Oneness

The highest spiritual emotion which is possible for you or any human to experience comes in those moments of deep exaltation and inspiration in which you have that glorious feeling of being at one with all the universe. When you have that ecstatic feeling of Oneness with God and all Creation, you have crossed the threshold which divides the world of sensation from the blissful heaven of Mind Consciousness.

You have cast aside the shell of your outer self and become aware of the Light which centers you. When you are in that spiritual state you are attaining the Conscious state of divine Mind which all mankind is seeking to attain, whether he is aware of it or not. The consummate state of spiritual exaltation in man is that state of ecstasy where the two interchanging expressions of love are no longer divided. They find unity and cessation from interchange through balanced interchange. When love is one in man, then man is Love as God is Love.

When a genius, or Cosmic Conscious mystic, is uplifted to that exalted state he knows that ecstasy which is the one unchangeable divine Mind emotion. He then becomes One with the Creator and his creations are enduring, for they are divinely inspired and have God in them. To the extent in which you can be thus exalted in your moments of aloneness with God you can know that state of ecstasy in which God's Mind is yours. Your creations will then be enduring because your thinking is one with God's thinking.

All people have great moments of baring their very Souls to the urge within them to forever seek that Oneness of divine Mind which centers their Consciousness. When you hear a happy child cry out its love for all the world and everything in it, that is its great moment of response to the Soul urge to attain Oneness with God. When you hear the whisperings of the forest, and the sweet music of warbling birds, the buzzing and droning of bees and insects' wings, and the majestic pounding of surf on great rocks and sandy shores with inner ears attuned to the Infinite, you are responding to that urge of your Soul to attain your divine state of universal Oneness. Deep love of Nature is an expression of universal oneness in man for it is love expressed universally. When man expresses love for other humans he individualizes them and measures his love out to each one in different measure, but his love for Nature is love for ONE. The Voice of Nature is God's Voice speaking to us His way and in His language. He whose inner ears are attuned to its mighty rhythms knows in them only the harmonies of God's love.

When Beethoven became one with the mood of the night he had attained Oneness with God's rhythms. He became transcendent because of his exaltation and he, in turn, inspires you to become transcendent and exalted. When a dear friend dies your deep grief at his passing tells of your oneness of love for him and for the world. Another friend is sorely distressed and love repeats his distress in you. A plane crashes with many people you have never known but the agony of your severance from them comes from the fact of your oneness with them. You feel that you have lost something of yourself. These moments of grief and distress are great moments of exaltation where love is all that is and all else ceases. These are your high moments when you are very close to God— and God is very close to you.

Many of our students write us that even though they have experienced flashes of cosmic exaltation they cannot hold that ecstatic condition, neither can they recall it at will. This exalted state, however, cannot be recalled at will for even when you find such heights you may soon lose them. Few humans can leave their bodies to become wholly Mind for very long periods, but one such hour is worth all the travails of a whole human life. It matters not whether this cosmic severance from sensation and Consciousness lasts but a moment, or for days, you will be completely transformed and know a power within you which you had never known before.

Countless thousands have forever asked The Buddha, and every sage and wise man through the centuries: "How shall I attain? Show me the way," thinking that if they are shown the way they can attain it by desire alone. To those who ask I say: Yes, the way may be shown, but *life must be lived to first manifest that which you desire to attain.* As you live life that which you *see* must be divided from that which you *know.* Each moment that you live you see many things, but in your great moments these all disappear. You then know but ONE. If then I show you the way it can only be by showing you the many things you *see* and dissolve them into that one thing you *know.*

If we look out upon the vast ocean we can see countless numbers of waves. That is all we can see, just waves, for that is all there is to see. We can count them into billions.

They are of many dimensions and of varying powers of expression in motion. That which your eyes *see* are many separate waves, but that which you *know* is that all are but one, each wave extending from every other wave. You see power expressed by these waves, but you know that the power they express is ocean's power and not theirs. Activity ceases. The countless many waves disappear. They withdraw into their source. You can no longer see or count them for they are the one ocean. They have found unity by losing separateness. They have found identity by losing individuality, as man, the individual, will likewise lose his individuality to find immortal Identity.

Your body and mine, and the body of every other man on earth, are each but one wave of God's mighty ocean. As we look about us we can see countless millions of seemingly separate wave identities. As we think out upon the world we are aware of billions of other identities which we can see, and count, and measure. Every one of those bodies is extended from God's One Mind ocean to manifest the power which is Mind. If it were possible for every living body, which is extended from God's One Mind Source, to return to that Source at the same time, the millions of identities of Nature's countless creations would lose their own separate identities and find their unity in the One Mind Identity whom they manifest.

When you look out upon the waters of the ocean you can see only the waves of motion which manifest the ocean. You cannot see the power of the ocean but you can know it as the one existent source of its waves. Man has looked out upon the universe through the eyes of his body for so many ages that he has grown accustomed to seeing separate and separable, individual bodies. Bodies can see only bodies. They cannot *know* them for bodies cannot know anything. They can but electrically *sense* other bodies. That is the first great difficulty which unfolding man must overcome as he gradually becomes aware that he is not body but Mind. His body has done so many things and expressed such great power for such long ages that he has come to believe that his body *is* that power. If his body expresses more power than another body he thinks of his body as being a greater individual than the other.

Objective and comparative separability is the fixed habit of human sensing, but sensing is not knowing. Humans sense planets and stars in the heavens—millions upon millions of them. Likewise, they sense countless trees and forests—blades of grass in woodland meadows— birds and bees and butterflies of the air—and fishes of the seas—and the countless insects and reptiles which impress their separate individualities upon the sensed-bodies of man. That objective and comparative separability is very difficult for the unfolding mentality of man to eliminate. *To think cosmically, however, one must eventually be able to dissolve that which he sees into that which he knows.* If you make the attempt to do that from this very minute onward you will be amazed at the increase in your own Mind-power within a year.

Start doing it then by realizing that this objective universe is not made up of many substances and things. It is made up entirely of electric waves of motion which simulate many substances and things which you have always accepted as real. The moment you fully realize that not one thing in Nature is what it *seems* to be, you are beginning to transcend your senses by your growing ability to dissolve what you *see* into what you *know*. That principle constitutes the difference between the one who senses by outward thinking to the one who knows through inner cosmic thinking. It marks the line of demarcation between the physical and the spiritual man. He who has passed that line thinks cosmically. He knows *cause* while he who senses is only aware of *effects* which he can never know.

The physical man who becomes informed through his senses sees and hears many things—countless many things which are all real to him. The Cosmic Thinker knows only one thing, for he thinks with his Mind and is empowered to dissolve all that he senses as effects into the one thing which he knows. He empowers himself with the ability to withdraw all thought-waves of motion into the still calm of the One Mind ocean which is the universe of knowing.

Recall with me now those many things which this radio electric universe has already taught you. It may be that we can look at them together with an inner understanding that will make you think quite differently of them. Look upon them as steppingstones which lead you to a greater comprehension.

Our senses tell us that there are many waves. We believe that there are many because we can count them. Our senses tell us that but when our Mind thinks cause instead of effect it knows that a wave never begins or ends. It is one continuity. If you sought the end of any wave you would never find it. If you traveled one million years at 186,400 miles every second you would be no nearer the end of that wave than when you started to follow it. It cannot come to an end. Even the waves of the ocean cannot come to an end when they break upon the shore. They but change their dimensions to harmonize with the pressures of space and continue on as waves of light pressures instead of waves of water pressures.

Neither can waves begin. Sounds, such as explosions, are the source of waves which seem to begin where the sound occurs, but factually, they only change the dimension of waves which are already there. Every point in this universe, anywhere, is the source of living waves of God's thinking, which never ceases to express God's thinking. The sound-wave you create has an entirely different frequency than the *thought* which caused that sound-wave. It can reproduce itself in space at only eleven hundred feet a second, while the wave length of your thought reaches out into space at nearly two hundred thousand miles in that same second. To demonstrate this watch a man who is half a mile away shoot a revolver to start a race. You will see the flash from the revolver instantly and then you will hear the sound two seconds later. At the very instant that you *hear* the sound from half a mile away, a man who is four hundred thousand miles away in space would *see* it.

These things you must know so that you can transform your thinking to be in accord with Nature as you KNOW it, and not as you SEE it. Knowledge vastly increases sense-perception.

Consider your own body as a focal point in the universe where waves have been changed in their dimensions by compressing them. You look about you and see other bodies like yours. You do not see anything between your body and these other bodies, but the space between each body is brilliantly alive with waves which tie you all together as one body. The whole universe is thus tied together as one pulsing intercommunicating body. When you walk among men you are walking *through* them. If it were possible to see the electric commotion you caused as you walked through the bodies of other men it would amaze you, also it would confuse you tremendously. The only reason you cannot see the brilliantly colored, rapidly changing electric effects, caused by the thoughts and actions of other people, is that your sense range is so limited that your eyes can only see wave vibrations between the ranges of four hundred billion and seven hundred billion per second. Below that range all the activity of Creation is invisible to you. There is not one pinhead size spot in it, however, that is not wave-activated.

God eternally thinks and His thoughts are eternally recorded everywhere. Every thought of God's thinking is repeated throughout the universe at the speed of thought —which is commonly known as the speed of light. This speed is not one of travel, however, for waves do not travel. They reproduce themselves at that speed.

You must also realize that wherever there are waves there are sounds, even in the blankness of outer space. Vibrations produce sounds beyond the perception of any living thing, but there is no silence anywhere save in wave fulcrums where motion reverses its spiraling course from centripetal to centrifugal and vice versa. Our human sense range is very limited but is increasing rapidly as our spiritual natures unfold. Our human range of hearing is limited to the range between 40 and 40,000 vibrations a second. Above that range all other sounds are as inaudible as though they did not exist. The world around us is full of sounds which no man can hear, and things which no man can see.

Every planet and star in the heavens has its own musical tone. The "music of the spheres" is not a poetic thought, it is factual. You do not hear it though because of your limited sense range. You look at a busy ant hill and hear no sound. There is a tremendous sound activity there, however, but your ears cannot hear it.

Those who have attained Cosmic Consciousness can clearly see the color densities which connect every object in the universe with every other object. They can see those stratas of increasing densities which so conspicuously surround all bodies, human and otherwise, with a glory of colors which rival the rainbow.

During my husband's great illumination of 1921, which I mentioned previously, his range of sense-perception so vastly increased during three of those thirty-nine days, that he could see the auras of people and things, even to seeing them in other rooms, and approaching his door from the other side. Also he could hear and feel the adjustments which the planet is continually making in vast slippages of rock strata yielding to changing temperature pressures, and ocean bottoms adjusting their depths to changing gravity pressures. These create great tensions which are threatening major geologic changes in our western prairie lands and in the mid-Pacific.

These illustrations demonstrate the fact that knowledge can come to one only from within the Mind. Increasing extrasensory perception will vastly clarify the mysteries of life, however, by making much that was heretofore invisible and inaudible come within the range of vision and hearing. The more you unfold mentally the greater your range of perception will extend. The time will come when you can transcend your body entirely and sublimate all of its calls by voiding them. All geniuses have so thoroughly acquired this liberation of body that they can forget it completely and withdraw its divided qualities into the fulcrum from which they were extended.

Mental beings do not have to be physical beings when they desire to escape from being physical. When they attend to the needs of the body for body survival they can become Mind only, and live in a Mind world when they so desire. The more you can look at Nature as One Whole, and yourself as all of all Nature, the more you can command what you are, to become what you desire to be. The more you can learn to work knowingly with God, from moment to moment, and talk with Him in His inspired language of Light, the more you can transcend your own body and command it to perfection.

In order to avoid the temptation and danger of becoming too scientific in telling you of the nature of this universe, a simple word picture of phenomena, which is very familiar to you, might better affect the trend of your future thinking. Recall that familiar effect which you know as an echo. You call into the valley, "Hello," and the distant hills call back, "Hello—hello—hello." That is radar. That is what a ship does when it sends out a beam to echo against another ship. If there is no ship there, no echo will return. Likewise, you may call your "Hello" across the prairies and you will not hear a responsive echo. Now why is that? The reason is that the sound waves which you projected into space continued to expand without interference. The rising cliffs interfered with their expansion and forced them to contract instead of expand. Their condensation brought them back to the dimensions of the waves you projected. The hills then projected them to you and you could hear them, for they again condensed as they re-echoed against you.

Give thought to this effect more deeply. Was it not your own voice that came back to you from the hills? Did you not, therefore, extend your body to the hills? The waves that you extended from your body are as much your body as the waves which are confined in it. Can you say, therefore, that you occupy a fixed position in the universe? You have already projected your body and your thoughts to the hills. They did not stop there. They reached our moon in about one second, our sun within ten minutes, and if people on any planet of Sirius could condense your voice they could hear it in about nine years. *If you fully realize this fact can you not fully comprehend that you and all creating bodies are universal?*

Applying this principle to radio, consider that you are listening to a voice projected to you from Japan. It has been radioed to you from there. Other people also hear it in other countries. You and those others are now the hills against which the "Hello" from Japan is echoing. The man in Japan is the radar station which has broadcast a beam. You, and those others, are the ships which his radar has picked up. If you fully comprehend this principle you are ready to apply it universally when I tell you that everybody in the universe is a broadcasting station, and a receiving station, for every happening which takes place in this whole universe. Likewise, everybody is an antenna which picks up every thought-wave of the universe. *You are in all things and they are in you.* The power which generates waves for you to broadcast is the Universal Energy of Mind-desire. The waves you broadcast are thought-waves. There are no other waves but thought-waves in the universe. Thought-waves emanate from Mind. Mind is universal. Thoughts are universal. Every thought of Mind is in all Mind, not in just a part of it. All thoughts are, therefore, in all thought-waves.

Your limited range of perception has led you to believe that your body ends at your skin. Your unlimited cosmic range of knowing tells you that your body extends to the farthest reaches of space. Your body is but a thought-wave record of your thinking, therefore, your thoughts and all other thoughts are one. They are universal, even as you are universal.

"There are not two separate and separable units in all Creation. Everything that is, is of everything else that is."

From The Divine Iliad.

CHAPTER IX

Application of Universal Oneness

The standard of a civilization is the mean average level of its constructive and destructive thinking. It becomes what it thinks even as one man becomes what he thinks. The world of man is still far from knowing that every thought and action of every man reaches through and affects the thoughts of every other man. Every good thought is like a drop of water added to the ocean's level and every bad thought lowers its level. A war-making, class-dividing, race-hating civilization is not the product of one man, it is the product of all men. No one man may say: I am good, therefore, I did not make it. He lives in it and profits by its conquests or suffers its penalties.

These are the lessons which are ahead of us awaiting our knowing. The more we can comprehend the Oneness of our universe the more speedily we may learn the lessons which will gradually raise the whole level of our civilization above the present low level of our man-killing, God-fearing, barbarian age. As that level slowly rises peace and happiness will come to man in the measure of his spiritual awakening.

It has often been said: "As a man thinks so he becomes." *Likewise, the world becomes what all men think.* Therein lies the answer to our present low-level world which man-thinking has created in our man-against-man world of today. To make a better world each man must change his thinking, by raising its constructive level. No man can do this beyond the level of his own knowledge, therefore, he must have more knowledge of the *oneness* of all mankind, and of the *oneness* of all the universe. He must learn to think universally—not separately. When a man knows that he is not a separate unit of mankind, but is electrically connected in Mind and body with all other men, he will begin to act differently toward men. When he knows that he is not walking among men but *through* men who are actually extended from him and he from them, he cannot help thinking differently toward them. Neither could his thoughts be other than those of universal brotherhood.

Children should be taught at a very early age that whatever they do to another they are doing to themselves. That is the very first principle upon which to found their morality and character. If they are made to know that they hurt *themselves* when they hurt another physically, or by unkind words, and are made to know it as a part of Natural law, that knowledge will become habitual with them. "As the twig is bent so is the tree inclined." Hitler said: "Give me a generation of children and I will give you another world of men who will be like me." The habit of thinking in patterns becomes traditional, then automatic. Mankind is more or less a mass of automatons. It thinks in the patterns of world traditions.

You should know, and you should see to it that your children know, the invisible universe even more than the visible universe. You should teach them how the invisible universe controls their every movement, governs their every action, blesses them for every expression of love which they give out of themselves, and hurts them for every hurtful thing they do. If the new generation is given that kind of dynamic knowledge, the whole standard of civilization will quickly rise because man's actions toward man will change as the patterns of his thinking change.

Many mothers now tell children that God knows everything they do, in the hope that they will be deterred from wrong actions. That is too abstract and too indefinite for the average child, and, therefore, meaningless. Nothing could so permanently hurt a child as to tell him that God will punish him if he does wrong. Children should be taught that they will punish themselves. Parents should talk to their children more dynamically and realistically about God. Teaching them to pray at bedtime can be as harmful as it is good, for many children think of it as a time to *ask* God for what they want without *giving* anything in exchange for it. The Santa Claus conception of God is not a good way to think of Him.

A woman once told me of the long list of things her child asked God for, which she herself bought for the child. "Don't you think it is cute?" she asked of me. "I think it is tragic, not cute," I replied, "for it teaches the child to expect things to be given to her without effort on her part. It does not convey to her the feeling that she must regive anything for her gifts. She should be taught to be worthy of every gift she receives."

Our students' children are brought up with a feeling of familiarity with the God presence. They are not taught to pray at prescribed times but are taught to talk to God at all times when His help is needed to guide them. To talk to God has the connotation of a conference or communion, whereas praying to God has the connotation of asking for some favor. One of our student's children came running to her crying lustily and seeking the usual comfort which mothers mistakenly give on such an occasion. The little girl had been playing with her sister and a quarrel developed. "Why do you come to me?" her mother asked. "God was there. He knows about it and I do not. Why not talk to God about it?" The child cuddled up in a big chair and was quiet for some time. Then she ran to her mother looking quite happy. "Well—what did God say about it?" the mother asked. "He told me to go and kiss Susie," the child replied.

That way of telling children to talk with God at all times gives them a friendly feeling of dependence upon God, instead of the feeling of a far-distant God who exists only to grant the favors asked of Him. They should be taught that they are either working with God or against Him. They should be shown by continuous demonstration how God works *with* them to bring food up from the ground for them to eat. How all the things they like, oranges, nuts, carrots, rice and all things else they need and like, are given to them only because God is working with man, and man with God, to produce them.

They should be informed of the manner in which God works with all of His birds, animals, insects, fishes and reptiles to teach them the way of survival through instinct. They should learn how God protects them through camouflage of their bodies which makes them more difficult to see. They should be taught the wonder of how God guides them in the choice of materials they need for comfort and of their engineering principles for constructing nests, spider webs, dams, ant hills, honeycombs and hundreds of other forms which are repeatedly done in every succeeding generation without being taught by parents. It should be equally demonstrated that these creatures all work with God as He works with them. They work to build their nests, and other things, as God directs them to do, otherwise they would perish. They do not ask God to do it for them, as many people do. They work *with* Him constantly, as all things in Nature do.

That is the great principle to impress upon children, for too many lives are wasted in wishful thinking instead of earnestly working. Those who ask God in prayer to do things for them without their co-operation are not *working with* God.

Many people say that God's gifts are free. That is not true. No gifts of God are free. Whatever God gives to you must be paid for by equal regiving. When you hear people say that God's gifts are as free as the air you breathe, they should be reminded that it requires an effort to breathe it in, and it must be regiven equally. Not even the life He gives you is free. You must regive it to Him. People often say that those who work for God should receive no payment for their services. Every man on earth continually works for God, whether he is aware of it or not. Every service rendered to any man should be regiven by that man. That is God's law. He who does not regive is taking. It will avail him nothing.

God will fulfill every desire of every man, insect, bird, animal or any other living thing, if he who asks immediately starts fulfilling that desire by his own action, with full knowledge and belief that God has also started working with him to fulfill that desire in the orderliness prescribed by the creative process, and *the time element,* which is also prescribed.

God will not "stop these cruel wars" even though ten million people ask Him in prayer to stop them, unless the people who made them start stopping them with Him. God will never do for man what man should do for himself—nor will He work *for* man while man works *against* His One law. When man works against God he hurts himself. He plunges his world into war by his own free will right. When he has hurt himself very disastrously he prays to God to stop the wars he is making. That is the great error of not knowing God's ways and making them our ways. Even though ten times ten millions pray to God to do for them what they should do for themselves, He will in no way work for them. God will fulfill the desires of all in His Creation, whether animal or planet—man or star. Not one thing is ever created without desire in itself to be created. All things in Nature which have no free will work with God as He works with them. Man alone, who has free will because he has Consciousness, asks God to do things *for* him without working *with* him.

Children should know that they have free will to do anything they choose to do by working with God or against Him, but that when they work with Him they find happiness, and that when they work against Him they make themselves suffer. Give them simple demonstrations of that fact at every opportunity. Show them that when they are watering a little plant and caring for its soil, God is making it grow, and that is the way they are working with God by creating a plant with Him. Then demonstrate that if they stop watering the plant or caring for its soil, the plant will die. That is working against God. Such demonstrations and teachings to children should be endless, and in all walks of life. If there is a great industrial plant in the neighborhood, they should be shown that it grew to its enormous size because someone desired it and started working with God to create it. It had been started by one man who had worked hard in a little place before he could employ thousands of men in a big place. Then show them the little sapling which becomes a mighty oak by working with God.

The present generation very much lacks creative knowledge and desire for creative expression. It lacks demonstrations, such as those indicated in the above paragraph. The trend of modern civilization and its teachings is causing far too many to expect public support as a right, instead of the opposite. Also the glory and love of excelling in work is being lost by far too many who watch clocks with eagerness for closing time instead of regret that they cannot continue to give far more than is expected of them for sheer love of giving.

These are the teachings which will make a better civilization because they will make better men. These are the lessons of Nature, our only teacher, which are of the greatest import for schools to teach. Instead of that our schools think that the teachings of greatest import are the dates of battles, the names of characters in events such as "who killed Julius Caesar" or the location of countries, cities or rivers. Any man may be a great inventor, painter or writer without any such information, but millions of children are bursting with such information who have no creative ability whatsoever, or if they ever have had, it was crushed out of them by brain building instead of Mind-unfolding.

One generation of teaching children to know their relation to Nature would go farther in advancing the human race than thousands of years of building encyclopedic brains. Moreover, every child's schooling should end at not later than fourteen, preferably ten. After the age of ten everything taught him should be by way of demonstration. Memory tests should be entirely eliminated beyond the necessity of sufficient repetitions to make mathematical tables and the alphabet automatic. Any educational extension after the maximum age of fourteen should be limited to professional training in law, medicine, statesmanship and the skills of the various arts and sciences. Every day spent in such training beyond the age of twenty may add to information but at the cost of lessening creative power. The ability to create can be multiplied all of one's life if begun early in life, but if interfered with during youth by formal educational processes based upon memory tests, it may be stultified beyond recovery.

I do not say this without vast evidence to support it. Practically every genius eliminated schooling from his life before the age of fourteen. Many pianists and violinists were famous before the age of twenty, and well known as geniuses long before that. My husband and I have demonstrated this principle. He was a good painter, musician and composer at ten, at which age he finished his schooling. At the age of thirteen he was a church organist. At thirty he had won world fame with honors from several European countries. During the last fifty years he has multiplied these achievements by a long list in art and in science. I also have had practically no formal school education which freed me for individual thinking and creative expression as a painter and philosopher who was not content with the world's unworkable philosophy. The knowledge which Nature and communion with God taught me you are now reading in this book. I feel certain that had I wasted my creative years in schools this book would not have been possible, for the years of making brain recordings might have made it impossible to awaken my own inner Light of Mind-illumining.

If we are ever to have a cultured civilization in which

the immortal in man is awakened, our educational policy, which now "educates" the senses of children, should be replaced with a system which awakens their immortality at a very early age through teaching them how to think and know the treasures of the Mind *which are within all men.*

CHAPTER X

God's Balanced Universe

God created this majestically balanced, beautiful universe in which man slowly unfolds into the heaven of eternal peace and happiness in the measure in which he comprehends the one great principle of balance in Nature. Peace and happiness can never come in any other way than through that knowledge and its application. Balance is the key to happiness. Balance is the key to all other attainment. It is the key to what we think of as *normalcy*. That which we think of as *abnormalcy* is a transaction in Nature which has not been completed as a balanced transaction. Unhappiness, misery, the agonies of war, the frustrations of life, the crippled and the blind, the diseased and the sick—all of these are not normal because all are the result of uncompleted transactions in life which leave a residue of unbalance in them.

Nature never allows abnormalcies to occur which will in any way upset the balance of the universe. To restore balance she will cause hurricanes to equalize opposite temperature and pressure conditions. She will cause a continent to rise from the ocean or sink under it to adjust unbalanced conditions in earth densities. The ocean bed itself is constantly undulating to equalize earth's pressures. Every transaction between the two electric forces of Nature is always completed. It begins in zero and ends in zero. No residue remains.

Nature is so completely balanced that the slight effort of a child throwing a ball in the air causes every star in the heavens to contract and expand in unison with the change of pressures caused by that slight action. Planets revolve around the sun with such completely balanced precision that their positions can be mathematically calculated for thousands of years ahead. You could point a telescope into the heavens toward blank space and prophesy that Jupiter could be seen at that point in the heavens a thousand years from now, and it will appear there on time—not one second late, and not a hundredth of a degree out of line. If our lives were as balanced as that there could not be a moment of unhappiness, pain, sickness or any other departure from normalcy in them.

Our earth has its own perfectly balanced position in space from which it never varies one second in a trillion years. It constantly moves to keep that balanced position, but it is moving in balance with every other planet in the system, which also must move in unison. If this earth had free will to do as it chose, as man has, and moved out of its orbit for even one hour, not one man would be left alive on it. The oceans would sweep everything off its surface in the cataclysmic disaster which would follow such a seemingly trivial event in our solar family. When the earth got back to its proper position, after such an escapade, the normal calm would return but life and growth would have to start all over again as the affairs of men have to start all over again after unbalanced escapades in their businesses. In the meantime the man or woman who got off their balanced path for a little escapade, which seemed too small to affect them, manufactured a lot of unhappiness for themselves. That is what I mean by saying that happiness and peace are impossible of attainment when people are out of their balanced normal orbits.

Assume for a moment that all of the planets in the solar system strayed from their paths, even just a little. Immediately their inharmonious co-existence would cause a solar disaster which would be like a cosmic cyclone in the solar family. Men do that, however, and wonder why they are unhappy and why there is so much suffering and misery in the world. When thousands of businessmen go off their paths by overoptimism, or greed, they bring down upon their heads a world depression or panic. When nations try to take from each other to enrich one by impoverishing the other, two violently unbalanced conditions are created which cause wars. Wars are effects of unbalance which have their *cause* in man, yet millions pray to God to stop wars which *man* created.

If happiness, peace, success and all that is good is attainable only by obeying the law of balance, the more we comprehend that principle the more we will be able to keep the human family in orbits which balance with one another, as God keeps His solar family in balance. For this reason let us return to the basic principle of undivided and unconditioned oneness in which balance itself is undivided. Motion is impossible under such a condition. Also effect is impossible without motion. There must be two extended conditions, which are divided from one, to make motion and effect possible. Witness two children sitting together in one united balanced condition in the middle of a seesaw. Motion is impossible, so cause and effect are impossible. When the children are divided and extended to the end of the seesaw they still cannot move for they are in balance with each other and with their fulcrum source. They must interchange with each other by giving and regiving to each other to create motion and effect. Two unbalanced conditions are immediately established which will remain unchanged if the equality of interchange is not varied. The moment that balanced interchange is not equal, however, disaster begins.

You can now understand that God could not dramatize His One Idea of love without dividing it, and extending it, and causing motion between the two by interchanging their divided love, as the two children on the seesaw were divided and extended for interchanging purposes. He created man and woman to know love, and to manifest love by giving and regiving love to each other and to all creating things. He divided man and woman *equally* in order that they might find unity in each other and interchange equally with each other. To divide man and woman *unequally* would be like putting a man on one end of a seesaw and a little girl on the other end.

He divided all Creation into equal pairs in order that all divided pairs could find unity in each other, through mutual interchange with each other. For God, the sexless Father-Mother of Creation divided all creating things into oppositely sexed pairs of fathers and mothers in order that they may unite to continue God's Creation by forever producing more fathers and mothers.

This God did to all things in His Creation—to all creatures above the earth and beneath the seas—to all the elements of matter which compose all bodies—to all the suns, and stars of all the heavens, and to the majestic galaxies which give birth to His suns and stars. The Oneness of all things He divided to make them appear to be countless many things and many ideas instead of but ONE. He divided them into countless twos, and impregnated them with sex urge to attain sexlessness through balanced interchange between the two.

He divided His Light into days and nights and made each one give birth to the other one eternally. He made the dark to give birth to light and the light to give birth to dark.

He divided His life into the life which comes with each inbreathing, and that other life called death by man, which goes with each outbreathing. He made life to give birth to death and death to give birth to life.

He divided matter from space and commanded that each forever give and regive equally that which each has to the other. Likewise, He made space to give birth to matter, through their mutual interchange, and matter to give birth to space.

He divided suns and earths into equal interchanging mates, and placed an equator between their hemispheres to balance their interchanging.

He divided His pure white invisible Light into equal red and blue halves, and placed an equator of pure white light between the two.

He divided the stillness of His universe of rest into vibrating opposed pairs of mates to create interchanging motion, where naught but universal rest is.

He divided His balanced zero of temperature into cold and heat, and made each to give birth to the other.

He divided His knowing into two-way thinking to create a balanced two-way sexed electric universe of interchanging waves to simulate the ideas of His imagining in moving forms made in His image.

Above all other things of import in His Creation He divided His unconditioned balance into two unbalanced conditions to produce effects of motion between interchanging pairs. He likewise made one inviolate law to govern and control all interchanging between all pairs. I will now give you that one law that governs and controls all motion in the universe which includes everything you do every moment of your life. And do not forget that you and I, and everything in the universe, are governed and controlled by that one law.

Do not forget also that whatever is wrong with your health, or business, or any other thing which affects your happiness—or world happiness—is caused by either your ignorance of that law, or by its defiance. Do not forget also that whatever ignorance you may have regarding the forces which control your destiny and your moment to moment happiness, is due to the fact that you cannot *see* those forces. You cannot see the invisible universe. That is why man ignores it, yet the invisible universe absolutely controls the visible universe.

You cannot see gravity, electricity, balance or truth, yet you are controlled by all of them. *They command you, and you either obey them and find harmony, or you disobey them and create discord.* If you defy truth by telling a lie you hurt yourself. If you defy gravity you destroy yourself. If you defy balance in any respect you punish yourself in the measure of your defiance. Whatever you do in obedience to that law, or in defiance of it, you are doing to yourself.

Herein follows God's one inviolate law which all Creation must obey or suffer the consequences of disobedience:

"My one command to all sex-divided pairs of opposites in all My universe is that there shall be balanced, rhythmic interchange in all their givings and regivings."

From The Divine Iliad

The unbalanced and disunited man-made world we now live in is entirely due to man's ignorant defiance of this one law of balanced interchange in the givings and regivings of oppositely divided pairs of creating people and things. Every ill which attacks mankind, or causes unhappiness, frustration or agony, is due to unbalance in his actions. Has that thought ever occurred to you?

If you are suffering from heart disease or cancer has it ever occurred to you that you, yourself, created it as surely as that you baked a cake this morning? You did it by defying God's law of balance in some respect. Nature is normal because it is balanced. Any so-called abnormality in Nature, anywhere, is due to unbalance. Your heart disease is an abnormal condition. Wherever Nature is given a chance she restores all abnormalcies to normal conditions of balance.

The secret of Mind healing lies in the power which is in Mind to command unbalanced conditions in people to become balanced. Jesus had that power because he knew the law. He could extend His balance to others because balance was in Him. He could command, because His knowledge gave Him the power to obey. No one can obey that which he does not know. Nor can anyone command who has not first learned to obey. Nor can anyone heal beyond his power to obey. I wonder why the world has not yet discovered this fact! There is terrible suffering everywhere just because of it. Everyone has a dozen minor sufferings daily because of it, and the world has the tragic sufferings of wars and hatreds of human enmities because of it.

Normalcy requires knowledge to attain and to preserve. The human race is very slowly acquiring that knowledge over its aeons of unfolding. The growth of spiritual awareness transforms humanity only a little at a time during each successive lifetime. You have heard it said that age brings wisdom, meaning that wisdom is the result of a life of countless experiences. If the cause of all the blessings of the world had to be answered in one word, that one word would be *balance*. Conversely, the one-word answer to all of the world's ills would be *unbalance*. Do you not realize then that the human race can only rid itself of its various ills, its wars, its degenerative diseases, its frustrations, failures, hatreds and minor unhappinesses and annoyances through long ages of countless experiences which teach wisdom?

From this point to the end of the book I will explain in detail why all of the afflictions which come to you, or me, or to all human beings, are due to the fact that we have not yet become sufficiently aware of God's one law to know how to obey it. We have not had enough experiences to become wise, or we have not profited by those experiences which we have had.

The entire lesson of life, and for ages of lives, is to learn how to equally unite the pairs of opposite conditions of Nature by equal interchange between those conditions which alone result in attaining a balanced state. Until you know how to obey you most certainly cannot command. And you must have knowledge in order to obey. When you do finally acquire that knowledge you will know the cause of your heart ailment and its source in yourself. When that time comes in your knowing you can then command your heart ailment to disappear. It will obey your command to disappear as surely as it obeyed your invitation to appear. It cannot do otherwise.

This new age which marks the beginning of new knowledge in electronics, is also beginning to comprehend the principle of Mind power to command matter, which Jesus alone knew and practiced with resultant certainty. Knowledge of principles, now being written herein, will vastly further this growing new power of man to heal, and to avoid the necessity of having to heal.

It might take many reincarnations of your body to have enough experiences to give you the wisdom and knowledge that you can gain in a few weeks by deeply meditating over these principles. If you will but think them into your Soul you will speedily acquire that power. Remember, however, that you cannot acquire knowledge through your senses. If you just read this book to remember it you will have but recorded pictures of the words upon your brain to remember and repeat. You do not *know* it, however, until you think it inwardly through deep meditation while alone with God. Until the wave vibrations, which electrically record information on your brain, have found stillness in your centering Intelligence, you do not *know* it. You have acquired no power through sensing any effect, because power comes only with knowledge. In order to help you to comprehend my meaning the following can be used as a key to aid your understanding.

You cannot *know* effects. You can only sense them by seeing, hearing, feeling, smelling or tasting them. You can know only the *cause* of effects. You cannot *see* cause. All CAUSE lies in the invisible universe, and all EFFECTS lie within the visible. You cannot see gravity, or balance, or energy, or truth, or God, but you can know them. You can see a sunset sky, and you can comprehend it, but you cannot know it. That which is transient, or in motion, cannot be known. The cause of anything cannot be found in matter, for matter is effect which can be sensed but not known. All cause stems from Mind, not from product of Mind. Likewise, you will much more readily comprehend the law of rhythmic balanced interchange between equally divided pairs of opposites by giving you some examples of the manner in which Nature obeys the law.

Remember the one fact that Nature never *takes*. Nature gives and regives equally. The important thing to remember is that the electric division of the universal equilibrium into pairs of opposite conditions is *equal* throughout all Nature. Likewise, her givings and regivings are *equal,* and in *reverse.* A balanced universe would be impossible otherwise. Consider your interchange of breathings. That which is given you to breathe in from space is regiven equally by your breathing out. Unless they are balanced you could not survive. The earth gives you your body which you must equally regive to earth. These must *balance,* even to a milligram.

If you throw a ball in the air you discharge the potential of the earth and add to the charge of space. When the ball returns it equally discharges space and charges earth. Likewise, the ascending ball loses speed as it rises to its highest point. When it falls back toward earth it gains speed in equal but reverse ratio. Like the borrower of money from a bank, the ascending ball is constantly being credited on one side of Nature's ledger and debited on the other side. When it comes to rest the transaction is completely voided by uniting the two unbalanced conditions as one balance.

Therein lies the whole secret of Nature's continuity. The rhythmic interchange between the two conditions of debit and credit are so balanced at all times in their equality that there is no resultant tension during the transaction or afterward. Each effect has canceled its opposite effect. Both conditions are unbalanced in relation to their separateness but each separate half is counterbalanced in the other at all times. When any such transaction is completed *it cancels out both unbalanced conditions.* Nature always completes her transactions. Her books always balance. There are no accumulating residues of unbalance anywhere in her transactions.

Man seldom *completes* his transactions in any of the many departments of his life. He is continually interchanging with many pairs of opposite conditions and hardly any of them are in balance with each other, or are ever canceled out. That is what is the matter with each individual life and the collective life which has made such an unbalanced world as our world is. That is why John Doe dies at forty when his normal right to live is eighty. In some—perhaps unknown—unbalanced transaction lies the answer to why Tom Smith was born a hunchback and your neighbor's child is "subnormal." Unbalanced transactions are recorded in the seed as accurately as balanced ones. Any unbalanced transaction which affects the seed pattern takes several generations to normalize. Very often God is blamed for allowing a child to be born blind when the cause of it may be traceable to a venereal disease in a parent—or grandparent. There is a beautiful tree in our garden with large branches on one side and stunted ones on the other side. Unbalanced distribution of sunlight caused that defect. All such "defects" in your life, and in Nature, have their cause in unbalanced interchange between the two conditions which have created them.

In unbalance lies the reason why your husband walked away from you. Every transaction in Nature has the connotation of mating, and mates must be equal for the products of matings to be "normal." All problems and unhappy conditions of man are due to a breach somewhere of the law of balance. That is what causes unhappy marriages. A happy marriage unites two unbalanced conditions into one and cancels out the two. Uniting two mates into one means simultaneously canceling out the divided two. When the minister says: "Whom God hath joined together let no man put asunder," he assumes by that that the two whom he has attempted to unite as one are equal mates. If they actually are equal mates God has actually joined them together and no man could put them asunder if he tried. Very few marriages are between equal mates, however. There are tremendous residues of unbalance in a very large percentage of them. In such cases God has not joined them together. They are still two, for unequal mates cannot become one any more than two halves of two differently sized apples can become one symmetrically and equally balanced apple. Marriage between mates does not mean that sex alone must be balanced. Humans have many pairs of divided conditions which must be voided by unity other than just sex alone.

Divided humans are lonely. Loneliness creates an injurious tension which is completely voided by companionship. Divided humans have innumerable pairs of divided interests which become ONE when united—and I mean *united,* not shared. When that great rarity of marriage between two equally unbalanced mates voids their separateness completely, they become united as ONE in all conditions, not just sex alone.

Let us consider other perfect marriages which Nature is so rich in, and man so poor. In a wave of water the amount of water which is above its level equals the amount which is below it. That makes a perfect unity possible when the divided mates meet and marry at the crests and troughs of waves. So long as that perfect equality of division between opposite mate pairs is continued, they will be rhythmically repeated. The moment that the slightest inequality between the two unbalanced conditions takes place, however, then the danger of a crash begins. In deep waters this will not happen but when the sand slopes up to the water's edge it becomes increasingly impossible for there to be as much water under the ocean level as above it. Continuity then becomes impossible and the waves crash on the shore as inevitably as happiness crashes in homes thus unequally balanced.

If your car gives you a smooth and pleasant ride you do not even think of your engine, however, you would immediately think of it if its vibrations suddenly threatened to shake you from your seat. If such a thing did happen it would be because of an unbalanced relationship between the two piston strokes which must continually unite their conditions and reverse them in order to repeat them. You definitely know that you could not continue to drive such a car. It would be dangerous for you —and would shake your car to pieces if it continued.

The most majestic example of a successful and harmonious marriage in all Nature is that of the interchange between those two opposite conditions which we call matter and space. There we find a perfection of balance which spreads out to infinity, without the slightest variance of balance between the vast suns and stars in the universe. Any marriage which could even approach "being in tune with the Infinite" would be the most unified marriage on earth.

Consider how orderly the planets revolve around the sun with such moment to moment precision that an astronomer mathematician can tell where any one of them is to the split second, or where they will be a thousand years from now. That is the way *God* keeps His home, and His millions of solar and stellar families happily in balance. Solar families must constantly adjust their own desires to harmonize with every unit in them, just as human families *should* do, but rarely do.

Every planet and moon in the entire solar system moves at tremendous speeds around the sun, but each one of them has to constantly change its speed to keep a harmonious rhythm in the entire system. The speed of the earth around the sun is never the same for one moment. It increases its speed for six months and then reduces it for another six months. Every other unit in the solar system does likewise. There are so many interchanging relations in these great solar families, which have no free will to violate God's law, that they would fill the rest of this book, but a study of them would tell why God's universe is eternally balanced and why man's families so frequently destroy themselves. It is difficult to parallel solar examples in human life for humans have free will in making decisions, whereas the stars of heaven are God-guided. They have no free will.

Man's opportunity for self-expression began when he first discovered that he could make decisions of his own without having to obey the commands of God's instinctive guidance. That is when he began to assert his "free will" for self-interest, rather than community interest. He chose to think of himself and what he wanted for himself without any consideration for the desires of others. He took what he wanted for himself by the might of his physical strength. He has not yet arrived at the stage in his unfolding where he has become aware that he is not a separate unit of Creation but an integral part of the whole. He still insists upon taking without knowing that his taking is impoverishing him. He has not yet learned that he can be enriched only by giving. He has not yet learned of his unity with mankind. He still has not learned that every thought and action of his must be for mankind and not for himself.

More important than all else is the fact that he has not yet learned that his free will to do as he chooses is limited to just that and no more. *He has the right to his action but God holds the right to the reaction—and they must balance, no matter what the agony may be to him who has to balance an unlawful action.* It takes a long time, and countless experiences, for humanity to learn that God is forever working with every unit of His Creation who is working with Him, but He will not work for any unit of it who is working in defiance of Him.

Human beings still think of themselves as independent, separate individuals who are in full control of their destinies and can do what they choose to hurt others without hurting themselves. Those who have learned the lesson that God is forever working with them are the enlightened ones who alone can save the human race from another fall, if it is not too late to save it. These are the ones who have learned that their own personal identity is merged in the identity of the universal Man whom he is. He knows that he is not of himself alone. He knows that all men and all created things are ONE.

That is the lesson which all men must learn, no matter how many lives they must live. That is the lesson they must learn about their relations with other men—but there is still a greater lesson that they must learn. *That lesson is how to find their own center of control while learning how to deal with other men.* That is the lesson man slowly learns which removes him farther and farther from the treadmill of mere existence and nearer to the spiritual power of Mind knowing, which gives him rest and freedom from life's treadmill.

The following are God's own words to man in relation to balance:

"I have but one law for all My opposed pairs of creating things; and that law needs but one word to spell it out, so hear Me when I say that the one word of My one law is

BALANCE

"And if man needs two words to aid him in his knowing of the workings of that law, those words are

BALANCED INTERCHANGE

"If man still needs more words to aid his knowing of My one law, give to him another one, and let those three words be

RHYTHMIC BALANCED INTERCHANGE."

From The Divine Iliad

CHAPTER XI

Man's Unbalanced World

Once again mankind must reap the agonizing harvest of the seeds of hate, fear, greed and selfishness he has sown in the heart of man. Once again he must pay in tears for not having learned that whatever you do to your neighbor you do to yourself.

God gave a beautiful world to man in which he could live in happiness and peace merely by giving happiness and peace to his fellowman. That is all that is required of man in order that he may forever live in the glorious garden of eternal bliss which the God of Love created for his habitation.

Oh the pity of such slow learning of the lesson that peace, happiness, love and prosperity can never be acquired by taking them from another, but only by giving them to him. How tragic that man should cast himself out of his garden of love by transforming it into a withering waste!

Everywhere in the world where man has sought wealth, power, love, peace and happiness by taking them from his fellowman he has impoverished himself with enemies who hate him. Despite the oft repeated teachings given by divine messengers that a house divided against itself cannot stand, man has created a world of such hopeless disunity that it is falling apart stone by stone, in spite of the billions that are being poured into repairing its crumbling walls. Disunity has multiplied so fast in fifty years that one half of the world is diametrically divided in enmity against the other half, and each half is armed to the teeth against the other half. One half of the world is free and the other half has enslaved its own people.

Wherever one looks in the world today to find love, peace, happiness or prosperity he finds it curtained by a pall of fear, dread, suspense, tension and suspicion. Legions of men are watching the skies with radar and electronic beams lest millions of men, women and children be hideously slaughtered in fifty cities within an hour. This is a picture of the ugly world which man has built within the beautiful world God gave to him. Is there any hope for saving it? Is it possible to transform its ugliness to beauty—its hate to love—and its fear to peaceful happiness?

Yes, perhaps there is. But the only way to transform this ugly disunited world which man has made is to transform man and his un-Godlike way of life to a way of life which is Godlike and Christian. To do that requires knowledge of what is Godlike. That means that one must know what love is and how to manifest love. God created man for that purpose only. Man has never really had that knowledge. He is not yet out of the jungle long enough to forget his primate days. He still does not know what he is doing even as those who crucified the Nazarene did not know what they were doing.

Let us, therefore, look at man's way of life and clearly show him why it is un-Godlike so that he may clearly know God's ways and try to conform to them ere it be too late. With such knowledge, and the practice of it in a lawful way of life, there is hope—the only possible hope —of saving mankind from another fall from the high point he unlawfully reached in 1900, and must now pay for. We can never remedy the sufferings he has made for himself by defiance of God's law of balanced actions by searching within the sufferings for their remedy. The only remedy for them is in knowledge of their *cause,* and the application of that knowledge to a lawful practice. The cause of all man's ills lies in himself. He has still to learn the ways of Nature and of man's relation to Nature. Nature has always had her doors wide open for man to know its ways and processes. It has been tragically unfortunate that man has passed the doors of CAUSE which made God's ways and processes eternally enduring, and looked only upon their visible effect with covetous eyes. It is necessary, therefore, to look to CAUSE in order to find why man's present fast decaying world cannot possibly hold together as a cohesive civilization unless he reverses his ways.

The basic answer to all human troubles lies in the one fact that man's way of life has been a constant violation of the one universal law which demands that all transactions in Nature must be balanced and equal in their interchange. Nature demands that every transaction between divided pairs of mates in the electric universe shall be so complete that each will cancel the other without leaving any residue of unbalance whatsoever. Every incomplete transaction in man's dealings with another which does not end in complete harmony and equal happiness for both, leaves a residue of unbalance which is best pictured by the word *tension.* Every trouble that the world is individually and collectively suffering from today is due to a vast accumulation of tensions which are as surely shaking man's individual and collective body to pieces as an off-center wheel will fly to pieces from fast motion. No moving thing on earth can withstand this greatest violation of God's law for too long. Sooner or later the ever-increasing tensions of unbalanced transactions, resulting from unequal interchange between mate pairs, will disintegrate any structure in the ratio of its increasing momentum.

Everyone is familiar with that principle as it works in simple structures, like a machine, or a friendship. If a tremendous vibration develops in the engine of your car you know that it will destroy the car, and you also, if you continue to let it accumulate its tensions. Likewise, your most cherished friendship will destroy itself if a series of uncompleted and unequal transactions accumulate until its tensions are irremediable. Everyone knows how family lives and homes are broken up that way, and how businesses become bankrupt that way.

A mass tension has already accumulated to such a dangerous state that, according to official statistics, one sixteenth of the entire nation is either in insane asylums or is a mental case. That is one way Nature takes to meet the tension of this fast world pace to eliminate those who defy her one law. Nature always has the last word for those who defy her. Her answer to such unbalanced world tensions, which man has created in the last fifty years, is sex-degeneracy and world-neurosis. These are two of the many conditions which are inevitably destroying the human race. They are but two of the fruits of an unbalanced man-made world.

Another effect of world decay is evidenced in male aggressive dictatorial power which gradually deprives the human race of its precious quality of initiative. Initiative dies in the ratio in which freedom in man dies. The suppression of free will in any country will as surely destroy that country as wars would destroy it.

How futile is man's talk about prosperity and economic growth in a world where men are multiplying tensions for a prosperity bought at the price of its Soul.

The world does not seem to realize that it is vibrating itself to pieces in that very same way by its fast motion around an off-center flywheel. The world's vast millions are trying to hold on to its dangerously vibrating structure with grim might. The tensions and many fears are multiplying degenerative diseases of the human body with increasing rapidity. To more explicitly clarify this principle of human disintegration it is necessary to view it from the scientific standpoint of Natural law. In so doing I will keep its science to child's primer simplicity. Without knowing at least the minimum which must be known regarding God's creative processes it would be impossible to either obey or command them.

The first step in gaining knowledge of the cause of your heart disease, or the world's heart disease, which is killing both you and the world, is to realize that we are living in a vibratory electric wave universe where tremendous tensions are developed by fast motion. The next step is to realize that the reason we are living in a vibratory universe is because God divided His universe of rest into pairs of oppositely sex-conditioned mates which must forever interchange with each other. If the interchange between all mate pairs of opposites are equally balanced they can continue a harmonious relationship and develop tremendous tensions which neither of the divided halves even feel. The moment, however, that the slightest inequality of interchange takes place the off-balance vibration begins to be felt and its destructive powers begin to operate.

Your heart vibrates very pleasantly if you are quite at peace with yourself and the world. If all your transactions of the day are balanced through friendly co-operation you will not accumulate tensions. Without tensions you will sleep soundly and dreamlessly all night. If your life is like that, you are sufficiently "in tune with the Infinite" to carry tremendous tensions without feeling them. You can never have heart failure or heart disease while living a normal balanced life. If, however, you begin to unbalance many of your transactions, you are accumulating a set of tensions which will eventually show themselves in physical diseases. You accumulate tensions in every dealing which is not a completely balanced transaction. You no longer sleep soundly. Your heart can never have one moment of complete rest. A hundred things are happening to your body which you do not even suspect.

In order that you will better comprehend my meaning consider the even swinging of the pendulum of the big grandfather's clock in your hall. That even vibratory swinging accumulates tension as the pendulum swings farther and farther away from its position of rest, and it loses that tension completely each time it passes that point of rest. The sound you hear is an even tick-tock, tick-tock. Suppose we now lift one side of the clock and put a small block under it. The tensions now become uneven. The ticking is unbalanced and irregular. The clock will no longer keep time. Its vibrations no longer cancel each other out as equal credits and debits at the bank cancel each other out. That is what you are doing to your heart by your unbalanced tensions. You have an uncanceled residue of unbalance left over from every vibration of your heart. You have made that condition yourself by forcing the pendulum of your heart vibration to tick unevenly. Your doctor tells you that you cannot live a year unless you can normalize your condition by complete rest—which means to recover your balance by eliminating your tensions. The whole world has the same ailment. It has accumulated a vast potential of unbalance which can be wiped out only by completely normalizing world-tensions by obeying God's law instead of defying it.

Now comes the question as to how the world can transform its practice of disobedience to obedience? This means, how can mankind start anew and work with God instead of against Him?

To answer this question we will consider the unbalanced transactions of man which have been the most damaging of his self-destroying practices. A study of these will show you how utterly impossible it is to build a peaceful civilization without working knowingly with God every moment of every day of life.

The greatest of these defiances of God's law is man's usurpation of power by *man* to make a man's world for man by suppression of woman. Let us now consider this fact.

CHAPTER XII

Man-Woman Equality

This chapter is addressed to the many advanced thinkers who are fully aware of the great world danger which civilization is now facing.

All such mystic thinkers also know that civilization need not fall if we but know how to unite mankind into one Being with but the one purpose of manifesting the love principle of Nature, instead of the fear and hate principle which he now manifests.

God's universe is *balanced*. That is why it is unified and continuous. That is why it will endure forever and cannot fall.

Man's universe is badly *unbalanced*. That is why it is disunited and transient. That is why it must repeatedly fall.

When grave danger confronts anyone, or the world, one wants to know what to do about it. If he does not know what to do to save himself he is helpless to avoid the danger.

World thinkers can save civilization if they know more about God's ways and processes which alone can save man if applied in time. The great cause of world unbalance is the disunity caused by the practice of inequality in God's divided pairs which He created equal. These inequalities are many. They could not be balanced in centuries—and that would be too late.

The principle inequality which is again destroying civilization is the man-woman inequality. That is the prime cause of world failure which *underlies* all other causes. That cause could be remedied in time to unite the whole world as one if world thinkers, both men and women, would do something about it now, right now before the next election takes place, and not twenty years from now.

The world resists change. It insists upon continuing the same old mistakes until the resultant suffering becomes too heavy. It has got to change, however, in respect to its man-woman equality or be self-condemned to another state of chaos.

The world cannot change unless individuals change. Each man must equalize woman spiritually in his own life, in his home, his business and his government. Until woman is thus exalted the tensions of inequality will destroy every civilization which man attempts to build alone.

Every woman should insist upon mental equality with men in all governing and managerial capacities, and when competent women are nominated for high office I am confident men would feel it their duty and pleasure to vote for them to begin equalization of international affairs. I say this because each time I have mentioned this man-woman idea to a great man he has wholeheartedly and enthusiastically been in accordance with this principle.

It will always be impossible for humans to build an enduring civilization until it equalizes its man-woman Mind power. If world thinkers would but realize that, they would be aroused to action in beginning to bring equalization into being. God created this world for men and women, not for men alone, nor for women alone. He created them equally as mates just as He created all pairs and all forces equally. This is an electrically sex-divided universe. The two electrical workers which create this universe are male and female. Each are equal. One does as much as the other in creating every particle of matter in the universe. Without that electrical equality in expressed force we would have a very wobbly, and dangerously unbalanced universe of badly distorted forms.

We will continue to have a badly distorted, disunited and wobbly civilization until men and women world thinkers begin to equalize the two sexes so that there can be a marriage of unity in the world which will produce balance in world actions instead of distortions.

Motherless children vitally need a mother. No matter how sincerely or eagerly a father tries to become both mother and father, he is never able to fulfill both necessities.

This motherless world likewise needs a mother. The father is trying to fulfill both offices but the more he tries to function as both, the greater is the disaster to the world family.

* * *

In man's primate days physical survival was of first import in his consideration. The necessity of fighting for that survival to procure food fell to the male. He was the strongest and more free, for children must be cared for while men hunted. Food had to be prepared and skins and rushes had to be made into body coverings. That part of the work naturally fell to the woman.

As the centuries passed, man, the hunter of game for food, quite naturally became man the conqueror of men for their possessions and woman became the household drudge, the tiller in the field and the slave of man, her lord and master. Man alone was free. Woman did what her lord and master told her to do. For long ages woman had no such status as wife. She was man's concubine— for long ages one of many concubines. Men enclosed her in harem prisons under eunuch guards where she was still slave among slaves and never a wife who could freely walk the earth like her master. And even when she was allowed to walk the earth she walked behind her master or under watchful eyes. Her value to man and her status with him was purely physical.

Man eventually discovered woman as a mental mate and took her to wife and consulted with her, but condescendingly. From that first step in the recognition of matehood of woman by man the whole status of civilization gradually rose to higher and still higher levels. The country which gave the greater recognition to the matehood idea of man and woman progressed rapidly beyond those countries which glorified man and suppressed their women. Likewise, every individual man who learned to love a woman because of her mental matehood with him, as well as her physical, progressed beyond all men who looked upon her as woman alone.

Notwithstanding these first discoveries of woman's mental worth to man, which made her more and more his companion, and freed her from man's guardianship, man still was the master—the lord—the one who must be obeyed—and that which woman gained in man's world was but a concession, not a right. When woman demanded an equal right to vote she gained only a concession as an appeasement. She never gained a right in man's eyes nor has she ever gained equality. She but gained the right to vote for *man*.

Pagan man made man the master of women, and ruler of the world. Even the pagan God concept was male—and still is. God, the Father, has never been the generally accepted Father-Mother of His equally divided fathers and mothers of Creation. Man the conqueror, the killer of man for the possessions of man, the pirate and trader in slaves, the exploiter and builder of empires, built this world in his own carnal image. He built it for man and glorified himself as the killer of the sons of man, while women wept.

Man has always crucified love on the cross of his own self-glory by the killing of men; and women have always wept at the foot of the cross, as they wept when men crucified the Nazarene while all but one of His disciples who professed to love Him, deserted Him.

All of this is quite natural. It could hardly be otherwise, for man in his unfolding (or evolving) remembered the fighter spirit of his primate days of taking, while not realizing that the woman spirit of giving was gradually awakening in him a keener desire for mental mating and the spiritual unity of the equal Father-Motherhood of balanced mating. The hardest lesson which man must learn during the long ages of his journey is that God made man and woman equal with one another in order that they should manifest divided love by equal interchange in their givings and regivings.

God's whole purpose for dividing His spiritual Self into pairs of fathers and mothers is to dramatize His Love nature by the romance of equal and opposite interchange of love. The romance of awakening love is far greater

than either its mental or physical interchange. Every expression of mating is empty without the romance of love
itself. Romance is love-awareness without which there
can be no complete happiness in any mating.

The Cosmic drama of Creation is a romance which all
mankind is perpetually transforming to comedy and
tragedy as it eternally seeks romance without knowing the
path which leads to it. Through the romance of balanced
interchangings of love between fathers and mothers they
find unity which alone gives to them the ecstasy of the
divine nature of God.

Physical sex interchange has been first in the desires
of mass-man. Mental sex interchange is rare, while romance starves in a world which would give all else for
just one hour of it. That is the lesson of life which all
must learn who search for the peace and happiness which
will alone bring rest from world tensions. The world
has never learned it because the senses of man have never
let him know the real meaning of either love or romance.

The world of divided humans must some day know
that God's divided universe is an electrically sex-divided
dramatization of CAUSE and EFFECT. The CAUSE is
Mind-desire for expressing static idea through interchanging motion. The EFFECT is what happens because
of that division and the necessity of interchanging.
CAUSE is, therefore, one—and EFFECT is always two.
The lesson of life is to learn how to so balance the interchanging between the two halves of every effect that all
EFFECT is completely canceled out in complete sexlessness by their balanced unity.

God's motive as Master-Playwright of His Cosmic
drama is the love urge of the mating idea expressed physically by the uniting of bodies to void the physical tensions

of the sex urge by balancing them, and thus reproduce other bodies. It is also for the purpose of expressing the love urge in its mental and spiritual expression by eliminating the mental tensions of separateness. This is accomplished by uniting spiritual mates for creating spiritual idea.

A mental sex relation is for the purpose of creating idea, while the physical sex relation is for the purpose of creating body forms of mentally conceived ideas.

That is why any woman and any man who have harmonious spiritual relations with each other, such as a mother and son, or good friends, or business partners, can multiply power in each other very much more than any two men, or any two women could possibly do.

That is why any organization which consists solely of men, whether it be an industry, a club, or the cabinet of the President of the United States, or of other organizations composed of women only, necessarily creates unbalanced structures in which there can never be complete unity.

That is why this man-made world is so badly unbalanced and disunited. Its male qualities are so preponderant that it has made a civilization which operates like a flywheel whose shaft is badly off-center. A woman-made world would be just as unbalanced. Its preponderance of female qualities would make it equally disunited.

There is no other motive to the love story of Creation than the mental and physical manifestation of the love urge by unity of Mind and unity of Body which can only be attained through balanced thought interchange—which is of first import—and body interchange which completes the unification, but is of secondary importance.

If you look into the life history of any great man you

will find a woman in it who had a tremendous influence upon the creative powers which accounted for his greatness. It may be more than one woman, such as his mother, and his wife, or sweetheart, or dearly loved friend. No matter who that woman, or those women were, the basis of their interchange with him must first be love *mentally* expressed. A spiritual union between any man and woman is of ten thousand times more value than love *physically* expressed without the spiritual.

Love is not objective, nor can it be possessed. The woman awakens love in the man, and the man awakens love in the woman. The romance of it is in the awakening, not in the consummation. It is the awakened ability to love which counts, and not the acquisition of the object which has awakened it, nor in any physical contact whatsoever. A woman may not even be aware that she is deeply loved, and the man who loves may never even exchange a word with her. Where love is spiritual it uplifts, exalts, enriches and ennobles.

Where sex is purely physical it debases and defiles. Millions have ruined themselves through physical sex expression which was not spiritually balanced. The roué is despised where the parent is honored. Whole civilizations have been utterly destroyed by the sex debauchery of incest and promiscuity. Wherever spiritual sex-mating is preponderant over the physical there is then the beauty and glory of the power which men and women can alone know who have that unity which comes to those "whom God hath joined together."

Any man and woman who are thus spiritually and physically balanced multiply their unified power by eight —not two. Two separate, disunited potentials are only two, but when two potentials act as one their power multiplies in the ratio of the cube. In other words, when two completely united, balanced mates act as one they do not *add* their two powers together to equal two, they *multiply* them in the ratio of gravitation mathematics, which are three dimensional.

There is no lesson so hard to learn, or of such great import, as the long lesson of learning how to interchange all spiritual and physical divisions of effect equally in order to unify them, and thus make two unbalanced conditions become one. A balanced life, home, business, community, nation or world of nations is possible only by learning that great lesson by the hard way of experience until it is put into practice.

An approximation of balance will not suffice for complete happiness. A man who still insists upon being "master in his own home," cannot have a happy home, even though he provides for his family generously and is a model husband in every other respect. With such a condition contentment is possible but romance is utterly stifled. A residue of unbalance still remains which makes it impossible to cancel out all actions and reactions by balancing them as a businessman balances his books constantly. A business could not succeed if a daily deficit made it impossible to balance its books, nor can a family succeed in being all that a family should where a constant tension exists which cannot be utterly voided.

The wife would try to assure herself she was happy by seeing the good points in her husband. Something would constantly be happening which would not happen if the home was a balanced one. A daughter might marry against her better judgment because of the tension which could not be eliminated, or a son might leave home where he otherwise would not. Unity cannot exist where tensions hold two apart. They will always be two until residual tensions are balanced. The two will then be ONE.

In countries where their women are forced to accept infidelities as a matter of course there can never be the happy home life enjoyed by those nations where infidelities are the exception and not the rule. Under such conditions unity is utterly impossible, because romance is impossible.

No great achievement of world import ever comes from countries where women are openly denied any approach to equality with men and they stand still for centuries. Physical interchange with women, unaccompanied with mental interchange, holds a nation to a physical level, just as it does with an individual. Neither individuals nor nations ever progress through physical interchange alone. Miscegenation ruined Greece. Thallic worship ruined many cities and countries while homosexuality, which resulted from such unbalanced conditions, created many a Sodom and Gomorrah.

Within the last fifty years countries like Turkey, Lebanon, Egypt, Iran and Japan, which gradually added to the status of woman by giving her greater dignity, progressed very rapidly from almost static levels.

The countries which have risen to the highest levels in culture, invention, science, industry and engineering are the ones in which its women interchange mentally with men as well as physically. Middle Europe and the United States have given almost all of the world's great achievements to the world, while the Slavs, Mongols, Arabs, and other Asiatic and African nations have given practically none of it. Whatever scientific, engineering, industrial or inventive advancement has come to Slav countries has been subsidized from Anglo-Saxon countries.

The advancement of women to mental esteem has been encouraging but there has been too little of man-woman equality in high places, such as industry and government. In these important departments of life the world is still a man's world, made by man for man, and in man's image. It is not a peaceful world, or a united one in any of its many departments, and it never will be as long as it is a man's man-made world. Until women become the acknowledged mental equal of man and share with him the executive management of industrial and national responsibilities, it will be impossible to have an enduring civilization of happy, peaceful, successful people.

An unbalanced civilization is as operatively impossible as it would be for a man to continually walk and work while even three degrees away from perpendicular. Wherever one sees world and national affairs being discussed and weighed for decisions which affect all peoples, both men and women, you see great rows of men occupying the seats of judgment as to how the world must act. Everyone is familiar with pictures of man-groups in such high places as Senate and Congressional gatherings, the great conferences of The United Nations, the international assemblies at world conferences, the English Parliament or the cabinet of the President of the United States. With but few exceptions here and there all these managers of world affairs are men, all engaged in making a man's unbalanced world which is as divided against itself as Man and Woman are divided against each other in a home where man is "master in his own house."

I am quite sure that present-day man has not given serious thought to this man-woman *equality* in high places—especially here in the United States where men revere their women so highly. I feel that those thinking ones who read this book, and remembering the great import of their wives in their work, will do all in their power to commence what could be the greatest movement the world has ever known. This action would be the spiritual rebirth the world is seeking and which all thinking men have been desiring to come into being to save it.

Our present state of world affairs is not in harmony with God's One Law. That means that the whole human race is endeavoring to build a civilization by working against God instead of working with Him. It is a defiance of God's command which Nature will not tolerate. Man *alone* can never manifest His Creator. Every creation of God or man springs only from unity—not from separateness. Creation stems only from united Father-Motherhood. *Man can no more create an enduring civilization without woman than he can create a baby without woman.*

All ideas of the Mind, as well as all created bodies which manifest Mind, must have a mother as well as a father. The great error of man in this respect lies not so much in selfishness and ego as it does to the hold-over of his pagan memory of woman's value to him as being purely physical. Until man and woman can equalize their mental relations and work together for spiritual unity, a balanced civilization is impossible.

We have long heard the hackneyed phrase that woman's place is in the home. To organize, beautify and manage a home requires a great deal of executive ability which women perform with great credit when they must do it alone, but gloriously so when mates work together. Women have been called upon in war emergency measures and asked to fill places unfamiliar to them, places which none but men have ever filled. They not only did the work with equal skill and merit but very often with greater efficiency than men.

When women fought for equal suffrage, one of the most familiar criticisms used to ridicule the idea of women as voters was the claim that they would vote for the man who had nice curly hair rather than the one who had brains. Then there was the ridicule of woman as statesman or as industrial director. "What would a woman know about government? What would she do in a conference of trained diplomats?"

Looking upon the results of our all-men world conferences since the end of World War I is it not fair to ask if the present dreadful plight the world finds itself in could not have been avoided if the balancing influence of women's spiritual nature had been present? Every man and woman must realize that it is not in woman's nature to kill, for her purpose on earth is to *give* life—not *take* it.

Our present unbalanced civilization is scientifically impossible to endure. It is fast disintegrating even now and its decay has accelerated very dangerously since 1900. It is so badly unbalanced in so many departments and institutions that any attempt to balance all of them simultaneously would not be effectual, besides which there is not time to do it that way. The most necessary and the most hopeful one of the unbalanced conditions is man-woman equalization.

This essential to world happiness could become a living flame which would illumine the whole world with a new light if every woman started immediately to "do something about it," aided by every man who believed in it. Such a movement can succeed only if organized into strength of numbers. One alone can do but little but if every *one* joined together in a multiple ONE UNIT of twenty millions or more before the next election, it might be quite possible to make the first great step in that direction by electing many women senators and congress-women, and even the Vice President for the next Presidential term. Such a world innovation adopted in this country would arouse the whole world of women in other countries where such an innovation would be impossible at the present time. This country should lead the world in this respect as it has in so many respects.

The way to do this speedily and powerfully is for you and every woman everywhere, to call a few friends together and form themselves into a unit of the Man-Woman Equalization League. It must be started by women but every man who is in sympathy with the movement should become an equal member of it. Every truly great man will immediately realize its import and become an enthusiastic working member of it. That UNITY is its very purpose.

Perhaps five other women in your town will have done the same thing the same day. You will hear of it if they have. That is news for your local newspaper. Then amalgamate and call a town meeting to become a Chapter and elect leaders.

When you have become a Chapter register your Chapter by its town name with this Foundation which will act as co-ordinator for nationalizing the movement.

Groups formed in large cities can register their many Chapters by district.

Other towns which have done the same thing will grow into County Chapters, then State Chapters in the same way that national Service Clubs like Rotary, Kiwanis and Lions have become national.

The appeal for this organization is so strong that its growth would become millions in one year *if every woman would but realize that women have the power to save the world from another chaos by merely asserting themselves as equal inheritors of the earth and of the business of managing all earthly affairs equally with men.*

When the movement has become national inspired leaders will be born from the movement who will strengthen it by becoming great national leaders. Then will be the time for issuing a publication which will be a power in affecting the votes of all the nation upon the platform of equal representation.

When women once realize this saving power which is theirs, and the responsibility which is theirs, this movement will become the mighty crusade which it ought to be.

The only qualification for membership in this new national organization should be a manifestation of belief in it by work performed in its behalf. A signed pledge of allegiance to a principle might be required for membership, but work performed and support given are of first importance.

It is hardly necessary to call your attention to the power which is vested in so many million votes.

Unless something of this nature is initiated at once we shall go farther and farther into the chaos which a man-made world is so fast falling into. It is scientifically impossible for peace and happiness to come to such an unbalanced world as this is, where the physical values are so preponderant over spiritual values. *We have either got to balance the Father-Mother basis of Creation or perish over and over again until we do balance it.*

I therefore say to every woman who reads this book: Will you start today to dedicate yourself to this world service? And I also say to every man: Will you help woman to give birth to this man-woman equalization movement for world unification and peace, and become a member of the Man-Woman Equalization League?

A tremendous responsibility rests upon the shoulders of every thinking man and woman in this hour of grave danger.

CHAPTER XIII

Basic Cause of All Disease, Sickness and Evil

A living philosophy should show a way of life that will lead to health through knowledge of the underlying principles of Nature.

A normal man expresses the joy of living in a healthy, balanced body. He creates his body in the image of his thinking. Through his thinking man either brings health, wealth and happiness into being—or the opposite. He makes himself what he is by what he thinks and does.

Financial, domestic, social and other troubles do not come to man, he brings them to himself. Likewise, health troubles do not come to inflict man. He inflicts them upon himself, through lack of knowledge.

We hear much talk about the great increase in such degenerative diseases as heart failure, cancer and kindred ailments. It is time to look at this idea which man calls disease in another light. Degeneration is normal in Nature but there are no diseases or sicknesses in Nature. Whatever is in Nature is a part of her normal processes, and all are normal and good.

All Nature is always normal. By normal I mean that whatever is happening at any time, or anywhere, is the normal result of law working normally. There are no abnormalities in Nature. An abnormality would be an *effect* that is not true to the pattern of its *cause*. That is impossible. A disease would be an illegitimate body or germ which Nature did not create or sanction with equal right of normality. All forms of life are normal forms. Diseased bodies would, therefore, be impossible, for all created bodies conform with Nature's law. There are no diseases in Nature, in the sense in which we understand it. Nor is there contagion, or malignancy or infection in relation to disease as we understand it. Every creating body in this universe is electric. Electricity cannot be diseased. Electric bodies cannot, therefore, be diseased.

We look upon a bad spot in an apple and say that it is decaying. We do not say that it is diseased. We look upon the bad spot on a human body—a cancer or tumor. We say it is diseased. We do not say it is decaying—yet the bad spot on the apple and on the man is the same. Both have other bodies which differ from their living bodies, but both are normal bodies. They are not abnormal or diseased.

The whole man and apple are not dying, but part of them are. The bad spot on the apple is the *decayed* flesh of the apple, but the cancer is a *living* body which is feeding on the *decaying* flesh of the man. The cancer itself is not a *decaying* body. It is a growing body.

Just as decaying bodies, like the earth, become living food for bodies like yours and mine which arise from it, *so is a cancer or tumor a living body—a normal living body which has been as legitimately born as your body and mine. And as our bodies are not diseases so are cancer bodies not diseases.*

A fruit fly which is born out of the decay spot on the apple is a living body which has arisen from the death of the apple, just as a living cancer has arisen from a dead spot on a human body. *A host of living bodies will arise from a human body when it is all dead. That is one of the ways Nature takes to return its givings to their source in order that their source may regive them.*

When you were born from the seed of life, the seed of death was also born in you. All your life those seeds of death wait for you to give them a chance to come to life for the purpose of living from your death. Even your mouth is filled with death-dealing microbes, which are helpless to hurt you until a sufficiently depolarized condition of your body makes it possible for them to find nourishment and multiply.

Your polarity—your vitality—your joyous attitude of Mind which multiplies the life principle in you keeps your body charged with proper balanced vibrations. These completely immunize your body from the chemistry of the death processes *which await your violation of life's processes.* The moment you do violate the life processes you invite the death processes to take over in the measure of your violation. A big violation, such as drinking poison, will invite all of the death processes to take over. Small violations invite only a fraction of the death processes to take over. Your lungs, your heart, your liver or some other organ, or even a small part of that organ, begins to die.

All "diseases" of every kind which cause your body to die in part, or as a whole, are due to the strains and tensions of trying to live. It is not easy to live a balanced life free from tensions. Our present-day complex way of living with processed foods and other circumstances, which are beyond our control, make it extremely difficult to balance all of the conditions of our daily living. This is a further reason why knowledge of God and His processes is so vitally necessary for all mankind. To live means to continue to multiply the electric tensions which multiply life-giving energy—and that is very difficult. It is very easy to die, for that return to rest is a complete relaxation of effort—but if your body does die Nature must take your body back into the ground from which it came.

Nature's only process of taking dead bodies back to their creative source is by creating tens of millions of living bodies within your dead body to destroy its tissues. Not one of these microbes or worm seeds can mature until you give it a chance by working against God's law of balanced rhythmic interchange in all of your transactions, within your body as well as outside of it. That means that you can live a full century if you know how to live and are willing to work knowingly with God at all times by making YOUR balance conform with His balance. However, you can hasten your own death and build a lot of aches and pains for yourself all through your life by working unknowingly against God. You manufacture your own "diseases" just as you manufacture the products in your shop. Your body is the product of your decisions. You can decide to live a hundred happy years by right decisions, followed by right actions, or you can kill yourself just as fast or as slowly as you wish, by making wrong decisions followed by wrong actions.

Each man is what he desires to be. He is master of his fate. He can make his own heart disease or his own cancer. He could not acquire either one of them any other way than by his own effort. God did not inflict it upon him. A germ did not give it to him. He made it himself. Sorrow, frustration, violent anger or hate started his dying in some organ of his body, or some spot in its tissue. Alcohol gradually affected his brain tissue. Nicotine started a dying spot on his lung from which a living body grew to feed upon his body.

How many living bodies are being nourished with your decaying body? How many millions of bodies are being nourished in order that they may live upon the red corpuscles of your dying body? Why should you be anemic? Why should you have abnormal blood pressure or heartbeat? Why should you have arthritis or colitis? These "abnormalities" were not in your seed pattern of growth to life. You invited them into your metabolism to hasten your death. Whatever you have thus unknowingly, or unwisely, done to your body you can also undo. The moment you reverse your thinking from its death-making pulsations to the joyousness of living ones, you reverse the entire chemistry of your body from overacidity to a balanced chemistry in which acidity and alkalinity are balanced.

Chemistry works two ways. These two ways are instantly reversible. One chemical action is positive. It generates life. The other action is negative. It is the radioactive chemistry of death. A beautiful, harmonious thought will cause the life-giving chemistry to vitalize your body, while an angry thought will immediately reverse the chemical workings of your body to the chemistry of decay and death. Your own decisions are what count—but you must have knowledge to back your decisions by right actions. Without that knowledge you may perform wrong actions with right intent—but the right intent will not save you from the effect of the wrong actions.

If you have a bad heart it is not an abnormal heart, it is as normal a part of your body as your arm is. *You created both.* The same thing holds good about the cancer. You created it but you need not have done so. You created it because you did not know how to command your body to live fully in all of its parts without changing its "normal" pattern. You have never learned how to obey the normal life-death forces sufficiently to keep them in balance. It requires much knowledge to learn how to obey the law which demands that you equalize all of your transactions. You cannot command them until you learn to obey them. You must learn how to keep your own normal pattern instead of changing it to another normalcy, which will kill you. If your ignorance of the law caused you to change the pattern of your body so that another body grew on it, or in it, the new growth is just as normal a living body as your own body.

That and the following are new thoughts for you to give deep consideration to. The ignorance which caused you to build a cancer or bad heart into your body, or a bankrupt condition into your business, need never have appeared if you had knowledge of God's ways sufficiently to realize that He is working with you to prevent what you erroneously think of as disease. If you now have the cancer and acquire the knowledge that you did not have while you built the cancer, you can eliminate it by reversing its growth process to a death process. That power of Mind to command matter must come through comprehension and not through wishful thinking, or not through asking God to do it for you without your co-operation with Him. However, remember this one basic fact, that reversals are instantaneous, but that the time element of eliminating the body growth is a part of Nature's process. It took a long time to build the cancer body and even though its toxic effect has been removed from it entirely by the reversal, the time element must be taken into consideration. That is why an emergency operation has to be performed on a body if there is not time to remove the growth mentally.

The more you know about Nature's mechanics, and the processes used in the construction of matter, the more you can command the body which you are traveling in. The chauffeur who knows little about his car has very little control over its troubles, but one who has full knowledge will not let troubles come, and if they do come he can command them to disappear—and they will obey.

This is the knowledge which is now needed to give the more enlightened of the human race the power of Mind to command matter. Nature's mechanics are also man's mechanics. Every mechanical thing man does has its exact counterpart in Nature. A motion-picture mechanism is Nature's method of growth. Everyone is familiar with a motion-picture projection machine, and its method of projecting series of pictures so fast that the illusion of motion is created. Everyone knows that these pictures seem continuous only because they change so rapidly. If the film is turned very slowly, however, you can see that there are blank spaces between each picture. In Nature those are the rest periods where the next picture of any unfolding idea changes.

The man-made motion picture has but few changed pictures each second but Nature's thought-wave pictures change over seven hundred billion times a second, which is the speed of thought. This principle is of the utmost import that everyone should know, for that is the way a tree, or rose, or a man grows. That means that the motion pictures which are being projected from the seed of you change their patterns over seven hundred billion times each second. That means also that you are not thirty years old, as you think you are, for not one particle of you is older than one seven hundred billionth of a second. Neither you, nor earth, nor suns of heaven, are older than that. These changing motion-picture projections of you are what make you seem to grow.

Look at the small arms, legs, fingers and fingernails of a baby. Think of the little bones in them. Then look at your own, and your fast-growing hair and changing blood supply. You think of them as the same body grown bigger. But how? How did they grow bigger? They did it by dying billions of times a second to be reborn again with more of the pattern which was in the seed. They did it by projecting new patterns to add to the old ones and withdrawing them for cancellation to again give birth to more changing thought patterns. That is why your small bones became large, and you became six feet high. That is the way a little green sprout became a mighty oak. You owe your nourishment and life to death. You could not live otherwise.

The oak tree unfolded from an invisible, ultramicroscopic seed. The seed is Mind desire. As the tree pattern unfolded from the seed to live the life of an oak it simultaneously refolded back to die in thousands of seeds of desire to live again. The traditional concept of this operation is that an oak tree is born, it lives a hundred years, sheds thousands of seeds, then it dies and its decayed body is returned to the ground.

We think of a man, and all other creating things that way. We never think of them as rapidly superimposed positive images which are being projected through seed negatives by the Light of desire in the Creator's Mind. That is the way the enlightened Mind should think of them, however, and when you do think of them that way you will better understand how the cancer pattern became as much a normal and legitimate part of your body as your eyes are normal and legitimate.

For a specific example I will describe one case with which I am familiar, which demonstrates how bodies, which do not normally belong to the man-pattern, grow in man's bodies.

Six years ago I warned a certain friend to stop smoking. Three years later this man consulted a doctor who told him that he would not live a year unless operated on to remove a lung cancer. In the meantime he was forbidden to smoke. I was not surprised, for he was a chain smoker. Within a year he died during the operation he himself made necessary.

The cause of that cancer traces back to the principle of balance which he so sorely violated. Once again I must repeat that people violate the law either because they are ignorant of it or because they defy it. In this case it was openly defied. He had been warned years ago of the danger, but nicotine had enslaved him by that time and he could not stop smoking.

It is interesting to know how the cancer body grew into his body. Let us analyze it step by step:

1. Every creating body forever repeats the pattern of its beginning but adds to it constantly as desire for addition increases. After millions of years of repeated unfoldings the various patterns thus developed from desires to live on the earth, or in the air, or in the salt seas, or fresh water lakes, give to Creation the types and species with which we are familiar. Each species constantly records every additional desire and every thought and action in

its invisible Source. These recordings take place billions
of times every second. The seed pattern constantly
changes because it is constantly added to.

2. All bodies must unfold in harmony with their patterns. They cannot do otherwise. Each pattern has a
chemical formula which has become necessary to produce
that particular type of body. That formula for man
includes many such elements as iron, calcium, iodine,
nitrogen and oxygen. Any other elements than those included in the man-formula, and in the proportions required to continue life, immediately reverses the life
process to the death process in small or large measure, if
those added elements are out of harmony with those required by man.

If any element is taken into the body which is not
harmonious to that formula it injures the body. We call it
a poison. A little poison can be thrown off by the body
but a large amount of it will kill slowly or quickly, according to the dose. We call them poisons because they
will kill us, but there are no poisons in Nature in the
sense in which we use the word. Every element is food
for some other element but is poison for others. Our explosives are made up of elements which are "poisonous"
to each other, which means that they are badly out of
balance with each other. All elements are normal and
good in their own harmonies, but there are many harmonies in Nature and all cannot be combined without
producing chemical discords. *What we think of as a poison to us is merely an element which is not in harmony
with the formula which creates a man-body.*

3. Nicotine is a chemical element which does not belong to the chemical formula which has been registered
in the seed of man for millions of years. A spoonful of

pure nicotine would kill a man immediately if taken at once. A very minute dose of it does not kill him immediately but it begins to kill him over a long period of time. Even one cigarette starts the death process. Even one cigarette or cigar begins to change the man-body chemical formula to another formula. I do not say "to an abnormal formula" for a new formula would be a new normalcy—but not the normal formula for man.

4. The new formula unbalances the normal one to such an extent that tensions develop and increase until they become permanent in any smoker's life. That means that never again, after nicotine has become a necessity, can any smoker fulfill the first law of Nature which is to so completely balance every transaction of his life that all tensions are canceled at the end of every pulsation. That foreign element which does not belong to the man-body formula prevents that cancellation. Its tensions cannot be voided. Complete rest and relaxation become impossible for the one so addicted to it that he is enslaved by it.

A man who is deeply worried cannot relax and sleep soundly for he is unable to cancel out his tensions. The nicotine addict carries those tensions into his sleep, into his business and even into his nourishment. The tensions of his cravings awaken him in the night. He must now add more nicotine to balance his new self-made formula. He reaches for a cigarette, perhaps another before he can sleep. He is nicotine hungry! Likewise, he reaches for more cigarettes while at work in his office because he is unable to think clearly until he has satisfied the demands of the new kind of body, and new kind of hunger, he has created for himself.

5. All living bodies are simultaneously dying. The only reason that any body of any kind continues to live is be-

cause it can sufficiently balance the two generative forces
which keep it alive to prevent the degenerative pair from
making it die. A simple example is the balance which
every living body must maintain between alkalinity and
acidity. If one keeps them sufficiently in balance they
generate life for a body. If that balance is badly upset the
same two will quickly degenerate it.

Life and death are equal. As long as you keep them
equal you will complete your normal cycle normally. You
will be able to cancel the tensions which will give you the
necessary rest periods between your active ones. Whatever
you do to unbalance them will shorten your normal life
period in the measure in which you unbalance them and
give you various sicknesses in the meantime. In other
words *you start the dying process the moment you give
death a greater opportunity to destroy your body than
you give to life.*

6. When you begin to die slowly by inviting death to
take your body back to the soil through ignorance of how
to live, you change the chemistry of your body. You develop toxins. Toxins increase as tensions increase. Toxins
and tensions are killing you, very slowly perhaps, or very
quickly, but they are as surely killing you as that darkness
follows day.

Toxins and tensions begin to multiply within a man's
body from the moment he begins to change the normal
chemical formula which kept his metabolism in a balanced condition. From that moment he begins to die by
*creating new life in his body which could live only upon
dying parts of his body.* He should normally have been
able to eliminate these dying parts in Nature's way.

7. What are toxins?

Toxins are the reverse of the chemistry that made you live and grow, which now want to make you die.

Toxins are the soured milk which was sweet—the decayed spot on the living peach—the fermentation of fresh fruit juice—the scowl which was a smile—the hate which was love—the carbon dioxide of your breath which was oxygen.

Toxins are the radioactive chemistry of death out of which the generoactive chemistry of life emerges. They are the death half of the life cycle.

Every toxin which will kill a man will also make him live if you bury its death into the ground for it to relive as life. Carbon dioxide will kill a man if he breathes it in, but if you bury it in the ground it will give life to plants and forests which will take its carbon for nourishment and give off oxygen for his life's nourishment.

Every living body has within it the seeds of death which are harmless in bodies when they are in balance with the vitalizing electric forces which charge a body in excess of its discharge. The moment bodies begin to decay, or die in parts, which means that they discharge in excess of their charge, all of the death processes await their opportunity to fulfill their normal purpose of returning bodies to their source of birth. New types of living bodies, such as stomach ulcers, tumors, cancers, goiters and many forms of growing bodies are born out of such decay. These are not diseases, however. They are normal living bodies which are born from decaying bodies. All of them have one feature in common which is that all of them live upon the parts of your body which are dying.

The decaying peach gives birth to minute flies and numerous other living forms. The seed of these other life forms is as necessary a part of the formula for creating a peach as the skin of a peach is part of that formula. If one smells the dying parts of a living peach it is a pleasant and wholesome odor, but the more it dies the more unwholesome the odor becomes until its "poisons" can nauseate one.

A more complex living body, such as the body of an animal, gives birth to thousands of living forms as the dying process gradually disintegrates the whole body in order to return it to the tomb of earth which was its womb.

The wholesome odor of living animal bodies quickly turns to stench as countless living insects and flies are born from its dead body and live because of it. One such dead animal body will develop so much life from its multiplying toxins that it could kill a whole village if not buried in the decay from which it came.

In a short time the dead body of a man or horse will give birth to millions of living bodies whose seed was in the man or horse seed formula, as legitimately as the pattern for the eyes was also there. Life cycles could not be completed otherwise.

8. Life forms are impossible where there is no decay. Each is equally necessary to the other. The greater the decay the more abundantly life forms appear. The decay process demands a balance between dryness and wetness, just as the life process demands a balance between alkalinity and acidity.

Dry deserts do not give birth to life in the abundance that wet jungles do. On a planet like Mercury organic life forms are impossible because its surface is dry, hot mineral. There is no decay there in which wetness is balanced with dryness. On our planet, however, practically its entire land surface is sufficiently decayed to bring forth abundant life. Old mountains like our Blue Ridge and other eastern mountains have many feet of decayed surface which will give forth much life. Our western and northern lowlands have still deeper decay, while the new mountains of some parts of the west are still dry stone and will not yield organic life for long ages.

9. Man-bodies were born into life from the death of this planet. Every life which the planet gave out from it must be equally regiven to it.

Life did not come as life alone. Nor did life accumulate as life alone. Life came in life-death pulsations. It came in the Mind-thinking electric pulsations which create all bodies. The electric thought pulsations which integrate your body are equal to the death forces which disintegrate it. They take turn, however, in one being stronger than the other. It is as though life and death are forever playing seesaw. That means that you are dying almost as fast as you are living for about forty years, then you die faster than you live for another forty years.

A healthy normal body throws off its death pulsations in a normal stream. Your dog can follow them for miles, knowing that they are your body. The perfume of a rose or violet is their death which they are likewise throwing off, and your sense of smell is keen enough to detect the presence of those dying bodies, even in the dark.

The smoker who has changed his body pattern by adding nicotine to his natural formula does not throw off his normally dying parts in a normal stream. Being unable to completely balance his living-dying cycles so that no tensions remain from one cycle to be carried into the next one, he accumulates those unvoided tensions until the normal human odor of his dying parts no longer has the wholesomeness of a human who is living and dying normally. Those accumulating tensions have now developed strong toxins which so vitally affect the normal chemical formula of his normally dying parts that his body odor is noticeably tainted with nicotine. His body has become a menace to the life of all other humans in a very small degree as the menace of a dying animal is in a large degree.

The nicotine infected body refolds its changed pattern back into its seed, for every thought and action of every man is constantly being recorded in his seed and affecting its pattern. At least three generations must pass before Nature entirely eliminates that fault in human structure, during which period the hereditary taint will affect the offspring of the smoker as syphilis does in a greater degree. The introduction of the smoking habit into the human race is a great curse put upon the race by man himself.

A woman who smokes during pregnancy will bear a child who will much more easily become a drug addict than one whose body formula is free from that taint. If succeeding generations of men and women smoked long enough, the seed would eventually accept it as a new formula. Body destroying drugs would gradually dull the Mind sufficiently to prevent its further spiritual unfolding until Nature restored its normal balance for man. That might take hundreds of generations. Nature works that way. She at first throws it off but continued desire for a different kind of body is a command of Nature to which she must yield.

No smoker realizes that the accumulating toxic matter which he has invited to become a part of his, or her, life is decaying in thousands of parts of his or her body, and that the stench of that decay can nauseate a sensitive stomach which is allergic to nicotine. If nicotine poisoning is distributed evenly over the body a smoker may complete his life without giving birth to cancers or tumors, but if the toxin of decay cannot be thrown off, the nicotine causes an irritation which becomes toxic, and the body cannot throw the dying parts off fast enough. They then decay *within* the body and become food for another body which grows from the dying parts of the body which are not normally eliminated.

The underlying principle is the fact that decay anywhere will give birth to life in some form. If decay remains in the body anywhere it will breed life to live upon it to destroy it. That is part of Nature's process of returning bodies to their place of birth.

Cancers are but one type of body which Nature generates from the tension-created toxins of human bodies. There are thousands of such forms in various animals but many which are characteristic of humans will not germinate in cattle or poultry. Many others which are characteristic of cattle and poultry will not germinate in humans.

That which is true of cancer is equally true of every other so-called disease which kills part of the body before its time. Toxins develop in blood, or skin, or bones from such tensions which could not have possibly developed if every transaction between body building and character building are always in balance.

Even a common cold demonstrates that principle of unbalance. The cold is caused by a difference between the temperature condition of a person and the temperature condition of his environment which causes a sudden condensation in parts of the body. No matter how much knowledge a man has he cannot possibly avoid having colds or various other ailments which his environment inflicts upon him, for no man has time to measure and weigh all conditions in all of life's transactions. Conditions beyond his personal control arise which cause him to unbalance his body strength. It is then his resistance becomes low and an unbalanced condition in his environment affects him. All the knowledge of a sage will not immunize him from the effects of his environment.

One might unavoidably be sickened by eating some poison-sprayed fruit, or devitalized by food grown with inorganic fertilizers. Under such circumstances environment makes man's control of his body more difficult, although he is partly to blame for helping his environment to hurt him. Knowing of these dangers he should at least be on guard against them, and also knowing that it would be difficult for environment to give him a cold if he had not allowed his body to become tired, he should not have broken the law in that respect.

Even the greatest of intellectuals who know the law, constantly, and knowingly, violate it. It is just plain human nature to do so, for no human is perfect, nor does he quite want to be. He wants to get something done *now* even if he is almost worn out with fatigue. That lays him open to many ills which could not touch him if he were vitally normal, but it tells us that we should never say to either saint or sage: With your knowledge you should not have caught that cold! The only answer to that is that he knows why and how he has inflicted something unpleasant upon himself and also knows how to reverse and void it, for he has the power to do so.

There are many other reasons why we cause our own bodies to partially die too fast for Nature to eliminate the decaying parts normally. We have described how the changed formula for a man-body accumulated toxins which decayed part of a lung and thus made a new kind of life imperative.

The following example tells of another way of accumulating tensions and their resultant toxins which have the same effect of helping mankind to die faster than he normally should. This example deals with emotional tensions of temperament and mechanical tensions of body abuse which mainly attack the stomach, head and heart. For better comprehension of principles involved in this example it is necessary to take a flashback into body history and interject some new thoughts which are not a part of traditional thinking.

1. If you were the general of a great army, or the head of a great nation with such varying temperaments as Eisenhower, Churchill, Hitler or Stalin, would you think that you could make important decisions and perform conspicuous actions without affecting any of your officers and soldiers, or any of your heads of government departments, or your millions of people of whom you are the acting head? Do you think that such a man is a separate and independent unit of Creation?

2. Can you not see the friendly feeling which would spread throughout the country by a Thanksgiving or Christmas message from President Eisenhower as contrasted with the hysteria of an entirely different emotion resulting from a dreaded message from a Hitler or Stalin?

Do you think it would be possible for your army of soldiers to be totally unaffected if you suddenly interrupted their peaceful pursuits with an order to go to war tomorrow? Would it not cause intense emotion and hysteria in thousands of families?

3. Will you now vision in your imagination the millions upon millions of people it takes to make up a nation and how long it took to build it from a few pioneers to a vast organization?

4. Now imagine the various cities, towns, villages, the roads and other means of transportation, the many conduits for water, and wiring for intercommunication, the power plants, disposal and manufacturing plants needed for supplies—not to mention the chemical laboratories and other departments—all necessary for just the mechanics of making a nation workable. Then add to that the management, or governmental departments which make decisions for this vast organization.

5. Now imagine something trivial happening anywhere, such as a fire in a small town grocery store. A certain number of people are affected by that incident, but not vitally, not beyond the immediate neighborhood. No matter how few are affected, however, a unified bond of sympathy extends from neighbors to the sufferers and aid comes from many quarters.

6. Recall what happened when the Lindberg baby was kidnaped. Do you remember how every man and woman in the nation became as one in sharing the sufferings of the parents? This tragic happening touched the hearts of the whole world.

These two questions have been asked to exemplify the fact that not one unit of a city, nation or the world stands alone as a separate and independent being. What hurts or helps one, hurts or helps everyone. All six of the questions were asked to liken a nation to a man.

The building of a man-body and a nation's body are alike in every respect. The man-body starts with a single

unit and adds more and more units to it until it has accumulated into hundreds of millions. During all of this
process God worked with man to fulfill his desires and
man worked with God to manifest God's powers.

Desire built the nation. Desire also built man in the
same way. The desire of one unit multiplied into the
desire of many units.

Over the millions of years desire added new parts to
the man-body here and there and everywhere, conduits
for arteries, insulated wiring for intercommunicating,
chemical plants for digestion, blood, sugar, adrenalin and
other body needs, an irrigation system for disposal, and
literally hundreds of other mechanical, electrical, chemical and hydraulic power systems. It is impossible to detail
the marvels of the human body which desire has put into
it, marvels beyond those of any man-made city or nation.

In a city an ambulance will rush to give first aid to the
wounded. In the human body a whole regiment of white
corpuscles will rush to heal the slightest cut on the skin
or stab in the flesh.

In the city engines put out fires when they occur, and
Nature quenches the fires of fevers when they occur in
man.

In the city ten thousand times ten thousand wires are
carrying messages over all the land as man's body does
every moment of its wakefulness.

All through the nation millions of human bodies die
and decay in the earth to give birth to millions of more
bodies, just as millions of leaves of trees die to fertilize
the soil to give birth to other trees.

The thought of first import behind all these questions and comments is the one idea of mutual purposeful-

ness and mutual interdependence of every unit of Creation to every other unit. The thought of second import is the effect which every unit has upon every other unit.

Why did God give man white corpuscles or adrenal glands, or elbow and knee joints with their lubricating systems, and a thousand other inventions for his body? He did it because man needed them to manifest Him. For that reason they are of vital importance to him, but in order for them to serve him he must serve them and keep them in good condition by supplying them with their necessities. He must especially keep them free from tensions in order that they can retain their normalcy.

7. Can you imagine a Stalin sending out a demand to his police for wholesale purge without it being accompanied with a wave of fear through the nation? *It does not occur to man that a fit of violent anger will similarly affect every one of the millions of units of his body which are serving his purposes.* Every gland in his body, every chemical laboratory and power plant will immediately feel it. Tremendous tensions will develop all through his body with the chemical effect of multiplying the toxins which are always accumulating from dying parts beyond his ability to eliminate them normally.

8. If you have a machine which is planned to operate normally at one thousand revolutions per minute and you drive it for long hours at twelve hundred revolutions, you are not surprised if it flies apart some day, because of the extra tensions and strains which you put on it. When your doctor tells you that you have possibly only one more year to live because of having done that same thing to your body, you wonder why heart "disease" should afflict you! When your machine flew to pieces you did not think of it as a disease, you thought of it as the natural results of an

overload. You knew that there was law back of your violation and that the damage to the machine was a breach
of law by you, and not a disease in the machine.

9. Every part of a human body is purposeful. Every
created thing is purposeful. White corpuscles were added
to the human body when they became necessary just as
adrenals and other glands were added to it as fire departments were added to a city when they became necessary.
These parts of the body are just chemical elements of
matter. We can very truthfully say that they do not know
anything, so how can calcium or carbon be affected by the
mental temperament of a man-body of which they are a
part?

It is true that they do not know anything of themselves
but they are extensions of you and they must serve you
as you serve them. They are electrically sensed to obey
you. If you cut your finger certain parts of your body and
blood stream immediately rush to repair it as the fire
engines of a city rush to put out a fire. Each must obey
the Intelligence from which it is extended. It must serve
its purpose and each is needed to serve its purpose. If you
hurt one part of the body you hurt all of it.

10. Your body is an electrical machine. It will stand
a normal load. If you overload it in many parts you throw
it off balance and build tensions into it. It becomes like a
wheel whose shaft is off center. The faster you turn the
machine the more it vibrates. You are the Intelligence
which commands the machine. Whatever unbalance there
may be in your electrical thinking is immediately trans-
mitted to your electrical body and registers your unbalanced thinking in tensions. Where those tensions in your
body are affecting it you do not know. It may be your
heart. It may be your spinal cord or your brain. Or it

could be your nerve system with reactions to your blood stream which would result in arthritis, high blood pressure, or even leukemia if the shock of vibration tensions is sufficient to reverse the generoactive forces which vitalize the blood stream.

No matter where the accumulating tensions create toxins in your body to assist in its death processes, the results are not diseases. They are the normal effects which either build or destroy your body, and both are good. In every instance where tensions develop toxins an extra strain is thrown upon the heart, the blood stream, and the processes which are continually eliminating the millions of parts of your body which are constantly dying.

11. Your body is a chemical composition and a workable laboratory equipped with complete apparatus for transforming the chemical elements which constitute a man-body into the chemical formula for the body as a whole, and the separate formula for its thousands of parts. The greatest error one can make is to assume that this vast chemical laboratory works automatically to keep your body growing normally. Even if it were constantly supplied with the raw material it needs for conversion, its entire processes will as immediately work toward accomplishing your death as they will for vitalizing you with life. Your body is not only what you think, it is also what you eat. What you think controls the chemistry which either vitalizes or devitalizes, and what you eat controls the balance between the materials needed for your body.

You may not realize it but pleasant happy thoughts make the entire chemical laboratories of your body work toward vitalizing it with life. Its electric polarity also multiplies its potential. Conversely, angry, sullen or cynical thoughts upset the alkaline-acid balance and make the entire chemistry of your body become devitalized. The greatest aid to balanced health is a continued state of inner joyousness. The state of God's Mind is a continued ecstasy. The nearer one can approach that state the more he will keep his body in balance and free from tensions. Let me again repeat that tensions are those parts of any transaction. mental or physical, which are not canceled out because of inequality in the transaction. Toxins are those residual tensions which have begun the death process in those parts of the body which have been affected by them by reversal of their polarity, which also reverses their chemistry.

12. Every emotion of your life immediately compels the chemistry of your body to strengthen either your life processes or your death processes. All emotions are expressed in thought cycles. Electric thought cycles must be completed by being voided. Unbalanced thought cycles destroy the body in the measure of their unbalance.

Happiness and a joyous disposition are impossible where emotional disturbances unbalance the nerve system and body metabolism. These produce food for frustrations and worries. The chemistry of digestion is thrown out of balance and decay of dying parts of the stomach supplies nutrition for another form of life which we know as stomach ulcers. If the residual toxins find a better foothold in the nervous system, brain trouble and insanity are the resultant effects. Institutions for the insane are being filled with people who have inflicted these disorders upon themselves.

Again I repeat, however, that not one of these effects are diseases. They are merely the effects which people create in themselves because they have not yet learned how to live balanced emotional lives.

13. There has been a great increase in "degenerative diseases" due to food processing and adulteration, and to improper fertilization. These effects, however, are not diseases. They are imperfect bodies which became that way through lack of the proper materials which the chemical laboratories needed to build a man-body according to formula. One might as consistently say that a typewriter has a degenerative disease if the manufacturer did not have sufficient carbon, tungsten or cobalt to harden his iron, or had to use lead instead of iron. When a baby has rickets because it was not given sufficient calcium to make it possible for its laboratories to manufacture bone, or a woman has a goiter from drinking glacier water which was deficient in iodine, or a sailor has scurvy because of eating too little green vegetables and too much salt meat, it cannot be said that these are diseases. They are but the *effects* of tensions which make canceled electric cycles impossible. Tensions thus developed form toxins which multiply the death processes instead of the life processes.

14. An entire group of diseases are those called infectious and malignant. Again I say, these are not diseases. They are perfectly normal processes. They are purposeful and necessary processes and that which is normal cannot properly be called a disease.

If an arrow pierced your body it would be called a normal effect, even though it killed you. If a mosquito punctured your skin and left another form of life in the puncture multiplying into millions which fed upon the dying parts of your body, that would be just as normal an effect as though a swarm of locusts descended upon your fields and found nourishment from your trees. If you fed enough quinine to these small bodies you would decimate them just as you would decimate the locusts with sprays and save your fields. If, however, your body balance was normal your generative ability to throw off your dying parts might be more than sufficient to immunize your body from the power of any infection or malignancy to affect it. All bodies which we call infectious are bodies (or germs, if you like) which live on dead and decaying flesh.

The Creator provided for the return of bodies to their Source with as much thought as He provided for their emergence. The return toward another life is just the opposite in direction and in electrical and chemical effects, but both are normal and equally necessary. In the chemistry of life every living thing you eat is chemically in rhythm with your body. Electrically your body is being polarized or charged, as a battery is charged. When the food you eat has been dead long enough to decompose, its chemistry multiplies its toxic effects. The same things which nourish you today could kill you if you ate them next week. It is called a poison if it enters your stomach but if it enters your tissues it is called an infection.

A happy dog could bite you without infecting you, but a mad dog could infect you if he bit you, for the chemistry of his whole body immediately reverses at such a time, just as the entire chemistry of your own body reverses if you become violently angry with hate. You also could infect another body by biting it at such a time, but you most certainly infect yourself by releasing the death principle in full force to return your body to earth. It may not kill you, but it could. It could give you convulsions resulting from your own poisons. Or it could find some weak part of your body and form a cancer or tumor there.

A smallpox, or yellow-fever germ, is a living body

whose chemistry is in reverse to yours. If either of them enters your blood stream it will find nourishment from your *living* flesh, just as a cancer finds nourishment from your dying flesh. If, however, you let those living germs die, and can control that process by inoculating some other body with them, their dead bodies will have reversed their chemistry to one which is harmonious to your living chemistry. If you then inoculate, or "vaccinate" yourself with these reversed germs they will destroy any living germs of the same kind which enter your body.

SUMMARY

In all this universe there is only life which has arisen from death to become life—and death which has arisen from life to become death. That is all there is. There is nothing more.

That which God gives to us we call life. That which He gives to us we must regive equally. We give our *lives* to Him. Why call it death, or decay, or disease, or malignancy?

There is nothing but eternal life in this universe and every action and reaction of motion creates life. That which confuses the senses in this respect is the fact that life is expressed in two directions simultaneously. Out of every particle of decomposing flesh life constantly arises in other forms, and out of every living particle of flesh death, decay and decomposition are arising in other forms.

The universe is eternal. It is immortal. It cannot die. It can but repeat. There is naught but life in this living universe. Just as the clock pendulum swings two ways to create time, so does the heartbeat of the Cosmic clock swing two ways to create life at each of its two ways. Life gives birth to death and death gives birth to life—and each is the womb and tomb of the other.

Likewise, there is naught but love in this universe of love which God is. The pendulum of love swings two ways in its interchange of love, but both express love and both give the happiness which is love, when the pendulum of interchange is equal in both ways of its swinging. When man unbalances the interchange between the two, and hurts himself in so doing, he believes that there is evil in the world to hurt him, and that there is good to make him happy.

Disease and evil are one. They are the creations of man for they do not exist in Nature.

CHAPTER XIV

The Science of Mind Healing

The science of Mind healing marks the greatest step in the spiritual unfolding of Intelligence in the human race since the birth of music and painting several centuries ago. As music and painting awakened the Light in man in their day to give birth to a higher culture, so is the Science of Mind command over motion hastening man toward his illumining in this day.

It has already lifted the whole human race one more rung up the ladder which reaches into the high heavens of omniscience, but the heavens are high, the ladder is long, and the human race is on its lower rungs.

This epochal Mind healing movement is in its infancy, however, and must grow logically and slowly, to be strong like the oak. Like the surgeon's scalpel which saves many lives it can cut both ways. It can kill when in the hands of the unknowing, as well as it can save when knowledge guides it.

That is the position of this God-power which one illumined woman placed into dynamic practice only half a century ago. It is true that she was instantly healed of a fever which might have caused her death. It is true that Jesus instantly healed men who were near death with leprosy and other dangerous ills. His healings were not miracles, even though they seemed to transcend Nature's normal processes. He had a power which no man has ever had nor can even comprehend.

It is true also that Jesus knew WHY and HOW he healed. Is it true that the thousands of Science of Mind healers of today know what Jesus knew, which alone gave him the power to reverse the death process to life? Is it true that they even comprehend what Jesus knew? It is true that Jesus said: "What I do ye can likewise do," but is it true that one can do what Jesus could do without knowing what Jesus knew and have his power?

Paderewski could have said to man: "What I do you can also do," and it would be just as true. But is it true that any man can do what Paderewski could do without knowing what Paderewski knew and gave a whole life in preparation for?

Perhaps it is right here, in the answer to these questions, that the Mind healing movement is not the mighty power that it should be after half a century of growth. By this time the Mind healer should have the status of spiritual doctor and be working in close co-operation with the medical doctor, surgeon, chiropractor, osteopath and specialists—each one using his special knowledge in co-operation with the other. However, instead of that mutual co-operation we have a pronounced antagonism born of misunderstanding of the great value of the one to the other. Lack of basic knowledge always brings a lack of appreciation and respect.

In our world of today one surgeon, one doctor and one nurse are worth more in a hospital, or on a battlefield, than ten thousand Mind healers. This is not as it should be. Each should be of equal value. The Mind doctor is vitally needed as a great forward step in the unfoldment of spiritual man. The science of Mind healing should be as universally accepted as the science of medicine and surgery. This is not the status today, for if it became imperative that either one or the other had to be eliminated from human practice by edict of law, the choice would overwhelmingly be in favor of retaining the Doctors of Medicine and Surgery.

When perfect unity marries the two branches of healing of unbalanced bodies, which have become unbalanced by unbalanced Mind decisions and actions, the mighty power which belongs to both will come as an epochal step forward in mind control of body, but not until. Such a marriage would be a great spiritual step in the unfolding of man.

The present antagonism which exists between these two benefactors of the race must undergo a complete transformation because they are not a separately opposed two. They are one. And there would be no reason for antagonism if logic and common sense were applied to the principle.

Every illness of man is both mental and physical, simultaneously. There is no ill of man which is just of body alone—or just Mind alone. The physical doctor is trained to cure illnesses of bodies. His basic assumption is that bodies are composed of chemical elements which affect each other, favorably or unfavorably, as there may be lack or oversupply, or of foreign elements which do not belong to the human formula. Upon this assumption he has long treated bodies as he would treat elements in laboratories. He thus gives pills and liquids to make up deficiencies, or dissolve excesses, or destroy foreign elements or germs which have illegitimately trespassed upon the body normalcy. It has never been a part of the basic foundation of the medical world to think of Mind in relation to body ailments. A great many of the very wise medical practitioners are becoming strongly aware of the Mind relation to bodily ills, however, and are taking it very seriously into consideration in their diagnoses.

Unfortunately this recognition of Mind and body relationship as the cause of all ills is not so generously shared by Mind doctors. If each branch of healers reached widely over into each others' fields of interest, as a husband and wife reach over into home and business affairs, the ideal of maximum help for humans in distress could be reached. Without that mutual sharing in a strictly mutual science the medical and surgical science will grow stronger and the Mind science weaker. Both are vitally needed, however, but only as a united ONE, and not as a separate and antagonistic TWO.

The Mind healer is trained to cure illnesses of the body upon the assumption that Mind is the basis of all ills and that God made man perfect. Upon this assumption a person who is ill can call a Mind healing practitioner on the telephone and, without diagnosis other than a brief description of symptoms, receive an absent treatment for the cure of that ailment. *God did make man perfect, but the body is not the man.* The body is a chemical laboratory contained within a marvelous, very complex mechanical, electrically wired body which requires a great deal of knowledge to keep it supplied with its necessary foods.

No man has precise knowledge of how to operate his own body. That is why it is continually getting out of order. A man may become ill because he gives his body the wrong food, or an insufficiency of a necessary food. The resultant illness is due entirely to lack of knowledge of how to operate his body. If he then goes to a Mind healer to cure it by the usual practice and techniques, the

Mind healer asks God to do for that man something which he should do for himself, and no possible good result can come from it.

God will work with man but not for him, and one of the great inconsistencies of Mind healers is that they constantly importune God to do for man what man should do for himself. If he has a splinter in his finger he must pull it out and God will heal it. If he breaks a bone he must set it in line for God to heal in line. Otherwise God will heal it as man left it. Mind healers who expect God to do man's part as well as His part leave many cripples to suffer through life.

I know a girl who would not go to a medical doctor or surgeon when she broke her ankle. She placed her entire reliance on a Mind healing practitioner. Consequently for years her ankle has caused her intense pain and the misplaced bone causes frequent swellings. God did his part but her refusal to do her part is the cause of making herself a cripple for life.

Tying up the broken limb of a fruit tree and setting the broken leg of a man are one in principle; yet man is not condemned for working *with* God when he ties up the broken limb to its normal position, but he is condemned if he works with God in setting his broken leg.

How often we hear healers say that: "If you have sufficient faith in God He will do it." It is true that He will do *His* part, but He will not do *man's* part. He will heal the broken fruit tree limb and it will bear fruit, even though it hangs to the ground. And He will heal the broken leg, even though it stands at a wrong angle and makes a cripple of the man for life.

You have undoubtedly seen crippled birds whose legs have been broken and have been healed out of line by

God. And you have seen dogs who were similarly crippled —but where man has worked with God and put a splint on the dog's leg it restores the normal condition and keeps the dog from being a cripple.

If you have a splinter in your hand—or a dust particle in your eye—or cut an artery—or puncture a tire on that extension of your body machine which is your car—or break a spoke of its wheel—or put your finger on a stove —you may affirm, or pray forever in faith and belief that God will work for you and remedy them without action by you, but it will be of no avail.

A woman who has a goiter because of drinking glacier water which lacks iodine must have iodine given in con- centrated form to make up the deficiency. The Mind healer condemns that practice on the ground that the ill woman is taking medicine. That is one of the greatest inconsistencies in Mind healing practice. They do not condemn a person for eating food yet all necessary medi- cine taken to balance body deficits is as much food as meat and potatoes are food. A Mind healer who would treat a goiter by Mind healers' technique could not possibly cure that goiter, for God will not do what man should do. A doctor who gave concentrated iodine and cured the goiter would be acting in obedience to God's law and the Mind healer who condemned such practice would be working against it. The doctor would actually be performing Mind healing because he was applying knowledge to the case instead of approaching it with faith which is not fortified by knowledge.

That illogical antipathy to medicine is one of the great- est factors in retarding the growth of Mind healing by preventing unity with skilled doctors and surgeons which would multiply the power of each.

A baby whose bones are too soft needs more calcium and vitamins A and D. It must have these or become bow legged, or worse. If a Mind healer deeply desires to help that baby she would give it calcium instead of absent treatments. If it were her own baby she would be as guilty for not properly feeding her baby as its own mother was. A medical doctor would quickly diagnose the case and give it calcium in larger doses than milk could supply in time to harden its bones properly. It would cure the baby, for the doctor would be fulfilling the law by working with God. The Mind healer would condemn this lawful practice on the ground that the child was taking medicine, instead of necessary food to repair a damaged body.

If a man has scurvy it is because he did not give his body enough green vegetables. When a doctor gives the necessary chemicals to a body to make up that food deficiency he is condemned for giving medicine, but he cures his patient where it would be impossible for a Mind healer to help him. God will not set aside His law. He will do His part in working with man but man must do his part in working with God.

Mind healers can be a great boon to mankind by dealing with mental attitudes which cause ailments, but where there is no unbalanced mental attitude, and they are called upon for what is purely a repair job on a damaged human body, or food deficit, they should either make that repair as a garage mechanic would repair an automobile, or work in co-operation with a physician who knows body structure.

There is a tremendous field for Mind healers in their own legitimate field. This need is everywhere, but the greatest concentration of that need is in hospitals, on battlefields and in homes and industries where mental attitudes are obviously the cause of distress. Thousands of lives are being ruined because of unbalanced mental atti- tudes. Frustrations are driving people to escape from themselves through alcoholism in this gloriously beauti- ful world of abundance and expressions of love in all things. Thousands of homes need not be broken up if Mind healers give loving service to these needs.

When a Mind healer changes one's mental attitude from discouragement to aspiration by awakening ambi- tion, he is doing to that one what Jesus did in giving a cup of cold water and a kindly word to the wayfarer, or what He meant by the story of the good Samaritan. When you awaken the Light of the Spirit in man by transmuting his anguish to joy, you are reversing the chemistry of his body from the death process to the life process.

That is what Jesus did in every healing He ever made. He made others heal themselves by extending His own balance to them to reverse their destructive body chem- istry to a constructive basis. This principle is basic in Mind healing. It can best be understood by the simple instantaneous Mind healings which constantly take place in life, such as the giving of your courage to a very dis- couraged man, or even in making a lonely and frustrated one happy.

Everyone knows how the old family doctor's cheerful assurance drove illness out of the window and made the sick one "take up his bed and walk." These are Mind healings, for they transform one's body processes chemi- cally from death to life. Doctors are, themselves, prac- ticing Mind healing more and more as they discover the healing effects of joy and happiness and their power in re- storing normalcy. It is the office of doctors to repair bodies, however, with their skills and knowledge of body

structure and the many things which can happen to bodies. It would be an untold blessing to them if Mind healers would join with them and effect work upon mental
attitudes while they work upon body repairs.

If they would do this the resistance which much of the
world has against Mind healings would be removed.
There is a great deal of justification for this resistance
which would also be removed if Mind healers always
worked with physical healers to prevent so many needless
deaths, due to Mind healers who believe that God will do
the things for man which man should do for himself. A
woman died, under treatment of Mind healers, who had
merely a stoppage of the colon. A nurse could have saved
her life in five minutes. There was no more reason why
God should have performed that purely physical action
than that God should have washed her face. God always
does His part but when man desires anything from God
and does not follow up his desire by action in doing his
part, God will not do his part for him. Wishful thinking
is no substitute for co-operative action.

Mind healers might take a valuable lesson from Luther
Burbank's method of healing a cactus of its thorns. He did
it by knowledge followed by right action. He worked with
God and God worked with him to do it. There was nothing of the faith and belief idea in his method, nor did he
spend his time in wishful thinking and expect God to do
his part of the work.

It may be that too much dependence is placed upon
faith and belief, instead of knowledge followed by action.
It is said that faith and belief could move mountains, *but
no mountains have ever been removed by faith and belief without knowledge and action.* Many mountains have
been moved, however, by those who had engineering

knowledge and of the skills and techniques of steam shov-
els, bulldozers and explosives.

The gravity of this exalted profession demands that
those who practice it have the required knowledge to
practice it. The clergyman needs years of preparation
after he hears the Voice of God calling him to serve man.
The doctor and the surgeon, likewise, spend hard and
earnest years before taking the responsibility of life and
death of other men. Even the genius musician, composer,
painter and sculptor who already have power within
them, give years of loving preparation to equip themselves to give out the power that is in them.

As long as Mind healers are attempting to repair damaged body mechanism they should either have as much
knowledge of bodies as doctors and surgeons have, or
work in unison with them. It is fundamentally logical
that every man must have knowledge of his own particular art or profession. It is as fundamentally illogical for a
Mind healer to attempt to repair a ruptured artery in a
brain by Mind healing techniques as it would be to repair
a short-circuited electrical generator that way. They must
realize that God will not change any *effects,* at the request
of man, as long as their *cause* continues, yet they accept
countless cases where they attempt to "cure" *effects* while
their patients continue the *cause* of them. That is as fruit-
less and futile as praying to God to stop wars while man
continues to make wars.

That is why more knowledge is necessary than the few
months that is required to secure authority to practice
Mind healing. Lawyers, doctors, engineers, painters,
sculptors, musicians, and pilots of planes need years of
training in skills, and accumulation of knowledge, to become proficient in their work. There should be no excep-

tion to this rule for so noble a profession as Mind healing which assumes as much responsibility for life and death as the doctor or plane pilot assumes. In other words of deep meaning, *no man can give out of himself more power than he has in himself to give.*

The entire case for the future of this epochal step in man's spiritual unfolding rests upon this one undebatable fact. Knowledge alone gave Jesus His power. He had the unlimited knowledge of a complete Illuminate. The fact that He did not diagnose the condition of a sufferer does not warrant a Mind healer from not diagnosing it for He knew the condition without diagnosis. It would be helpful to the growth of Mind healing to relate some of the things which He knew that gave Him his power. To demonstrate how much He had to give out of Himself I will tell you three things He knew which are unknown even to this day.

1. He knew that there is an entirely different chemical action to the generoactive electrical pulsation which polarizes and vitalizes bodies into life than the chemical reaction of the radioactive pulsation which depolarizes and devitalizes bodies toward death. He was thoroughly aware of the construction of matter in this curved wave universe. He knew that the multiplication of power to vitalize matter into stronger life was electrically expressed (centripetally) in the spiral direction of gravity, and that the opposite (centrifugal) spiral direction led to disappearance in death. Knowing how to obey these two opposing processes by living in conformity with them, He could command them to reflect His image in them.

He thoroughly comprehended that a reversal of the death process would cause an instantaneous "healing" of anything which is dying, by making it live. He knew the electrical nature of that process, which is a forever turning inside-out and outside-in series of centrifugal and centripetal interchangings which compress and expand sequentially. His instantaneous healings are proof that he not only knew the process but could command it.

2. He knew that perfect mental and physical balance is impossible without perfect symmetry. There are only two perfectly symmetrical forms in Nature—the cube and the sphere. All other forms are sections or multiples of these two forms. God made the sphere for the physical universe and the cube for the invisible universe, which is divided into wave fields of cubic form. He knew that every normal healthy body is composed of perfect spheres and that the symmetry of those spheres is controlled by the polarity of invisible cubic wave fields. A human body is composed of countless billions of spheres, as perfect in shape as our sun is perfect, if the body is vital and alive. If the body becomes devitalized these spheres begin to flatten like our earth which has begun to die. When that happens the chemistry of death reverses the chemistry of life. The symmetry of the sphere begins to change to the symmetry of the spheroid and the ellipse. The cube symmetry which controls the sphere now lengthens gradually until the cube entirely flattens and disappears into the zero stillness of its birth. When that happens the chemistry of death takes over from the chemistry of life. Cube symmetry is no longer possible. That means that the billions of spheres which comprise a vital body begin to flatten and wobble on their axes like dying tops.

His knowledge of such processes in the construction of living and dying matter gave Him the power to extend His own balance to the unbalanced one and reverse his polarity from the direction of death to the direction of life.

He did this by becoming one in Mind with the one he healed. He who was ill thus healed himself. *No one can heal another. He can but make the other heal himself by reversing his thinking.*

3. Jesus had the full range of extrasensory perception. He did not need to diagnose a case for that reason. He thoroughly knew the nature of the ailment and its cause without questioning the ailing one for symptoms, better than the most skilled doctor could ascertain them by the many methods used for that purpose. He could diagnose an ailment of a person at a distance, even though He had never known him, as well as though the man were present. Moreover He knew the thoughts of anyone, anywhere, upon whom He might focus.

There has been one case of extrasensory perception in recent human history, of a man who could diagnose symptoms of ailments of distant, unknown people, but during the periods of such diagnoses, the normal sense range was sacrificed to make the extended range possible. This man was Edward Cayce of Virginia. Hundreds of names and addresses of men in different cities were given to him. In each case he severed his seat of sensation from his Consciousness sufficiently to project his conscious awareness to that person and dictate a complete analysis of the ailment. In every case the diagnoses he gave was found to be accurate. Some may have been incomplete, but that which he gave was always accurate. The condition he was in while losing a personal sense of existence was what is known as the trance state.

The knowledge which Jesus had, as partially given above, will some day be taught in the schools which graduate those who desire to emulate Jesus. It is necessary knowledge to have in order to perform such seemingly miraculous healings as those He made. To the best of one's ability, one should acquire as much knowledge as possible of God and His ways and processes of Creation under His Mind control. An earnest application of whatever knowledge one can acquire, however, will make it possible to make marvelous healings of such a nature that one may fully comprehend the *cause* as well as the *effect*.

Man should be taught what he should do for himself. God will work with a man who desires a potato crop by using all the power of His universe in growing and ripening the seed which man puts into the earth, but God will not put the seed into the earth. Every service which man gives in planting the seed and cultivating the soil, God will match equally by making the seed grow into fruition.

Man must thus work with God in the care of his own body. He must provide food for his body, put it into his mouth and masticate it. God will supply the mechanism for digesting it and converting it into blood, but He will not do both. Likewise, man must do everything which is physical effort to take care of the body mechanism by nourishing it, cleaning it, giving it necessary exercise and repairing it. God will do His part of the healing of wounds, digestion of foods, and other creative necessities of growth, but He will not fill one's teeth, wash one's face, make eyeglasses for him, set his broken bones or any such service that man should do for himself. It is readily understandable, though, how commonly this fundamental is ignored by people who expect that God will do *both* parts.

I feel that this new spiritual unfolding is still so new that many more things should be explained which are extraneous to the purpose of this book, but the mystery of what is known as instantaneous healings should be more succinctly clarified, lest a lack of understanding may lead to believing that it means that cancer or leprous scales will immediately drop off the body if they are instantly healed. When any foreign body, which is living upon the dying flesh of a living man, is destroyed by reversing the chemistry of the man, Nature gradually eliminates the dead particles. It takes time to "grow" them off in the reverse process of their growing on. They are no longer living, however, and can no longer be nourished by man's body. All changes in Nature follow the process of integration and disintegration by the motion-picture technique of projecting one changing picture after another into a living body to integrate it, or into space to disintegrate it. The time element is as imperative one way as the other.

Scales on a tree are a more familiar example. When the tree is sprayed the chemistry of the scales is reversed instantly, but it may take weeks for the scales to disappear. This explains instantaneous healings in bodies which are damaged by other than their own normal growths. If the Mind healer understands the conditions he can command that "abnormal" body to disappear by changing the attitude of Mind of the patient so that he can heal himself, if there is time left to do it. Even though an instantaneous healing can take place the body can eliminate just so much and no more. The surgeon should then remove it, but how often he will say: "If you had only come two years ago this operation would not have been necessary."

As a contrast to this kind of healing, where a surgeon *should* co-operate with the practitioner, I will describe an instantaneous healing where a man was near death without having any discernible physical ailment.

As a precedent to this story I repeat two salient facts which apply to all such healings:

1. *A man becomes what he thinks. He is constantly re-making himself into his own image.*

This means exactly what it says. Every thought and action, from one moment to the next, is instantly recorded upon his body and changes it constantly to the pattern of every changing mental attitude. A joyful attitude of Mind brings a smile to one's face to tell the world of the change from two minutes before, when he may have had an impatient or even angry attitude. Every changing attitude of Mind immediately affects the chemistry of his body. It simultaneously starts to work changing the man's body to conform to his own changing image.

2. *Every man can command matter in the measure of his ability to obey the laws governing the construction of matter.*

This also means exactly what it says. Our power is limited to our knowledge of the Source of power and the law governing the balanced interchange between the two expressions of that power. It means also that we can extend our own power to others in the measure that we have it to give, and in the limited measure of their desire to have what we have to give. To command matter means to reflect our power to it so that it reflects our image in it. *It then becomes what we think, as we become what we think.*

And now for the story which demonstrates the above principles.

A surgeon told a patient that he would surely die unless he was operated upon within a year, and even then he could give but little assurance that he could survive the operation.

"If you think I might die by the operation, and I have about a year to live, and as you mentioned your belief in prayer, do you think that I would have a chance to live if I prayed?" the patient asked.

"I am more and more inclined to believe that you could, *if you know how to pray*. Many of us doctors and surgeons see so many things happen to patients whom we give up that we are beginning to feel that there is much beyond our physical bodies which we do not understand. I will tell you of one of my own cases.

"I had a man patient who was so near death that we expected it hourly. What is more, he did not seem to want to live, for he gave every symptom of being in utter despair. He had not touched food for three days, and when he last tried he could not keep it down. Then a strange thing happened. A woman came in and cried over him and went away. Two hours later that dying man sat up in bed and asked for food.

" 'What miracle is this?' I asked of him.

" 'It is no miracle at all,' he replied in a strong voice. 'My wife wants me to live—says she loves me and will come back to me if I will live. So now I want to live. Until now I wanted to die.'

"I have seen so many things like that happen to those we doctors have given up, that I suggested it to you, whom I had also given up.

"I told you also that you must know how to pray, although this man did not pray, nor did his wife pray, or at least I did not see her pray. When she left, however, he became instantly reborn to life instead of being close to death.

"I believe that the power of love was at the bottom of it somehow. While he was in despair he was really a very ill man, but hope and happiness made him well instantly. We have no medicine or process which will do that. I cannot understand it. I would give much to be able to comprehend what really happened."

What actually happened was that the wife transferred the love which was in balance in her to her husband to restore his balance, therefore reversing his desire to die to a desire to live. This immediately caused a reversal of his body chemistry which always builds a body in the image of the thinker.

This is the underlying principle of all of Jesus's healings for He made others to heal themselves by extending His balance to them.

Love is a moment to moment wordless prayer, for it is desire expressed in silent communion with God. Desire of Mind is the only energy in the universe. Desire to live is manifested in motion by the polarizing force of vitalized action. Desire for rest from action is equally strong, however, and is manifested by cessation of action. That is what we so erroneously think of as death. There is no death in God's living universe. *There is naught but Life in action and also in the rest—which man calls Death.*

CHAPTER XV

Where Do I Go When I Die?

Death has been the greatest mystery of the ages. "Where do I go when I die?" is one of the great unsolved questions of the ages. Since early pagan days the after-death condition of man has caused many false concepts to come into being regarding this question. These many primitive and pagan conceptions, inherited from primate days, have never been modified because of lack of real knowledge among the masses. Intellectual, scientific and cultural people have cleansed their minds of such thinking but have never substituted another logical or scientific answer to replace the old pagan concepts.

Let us give consideration to this question and demonstrate that there is no basis whatsoever for these ancient pagan beliefs of after-death identities of bodies. Every one of these various concepts is founded on the false premise that the *body* is the person, the identity, the being. As the body is not the person, or the identity, these conceptions fall apart by sheer logic.

The question: "Where do I go when I die?" has two answers. It has one answer for the idea that the body is the person, and another answer for the idea that the Mind is the person. Let us answer the last question first. The answer is that you do not die. You are a Soul—which is a unit idea of immortal Mind. You are an Identity within The Universal Oneness, but you are that Oneness. You are the thinking of the Thinker who centers a body which records the thoughts of the Thinker.

You are desire in Mind to manifest Mind. You are the Universe, manifesting the whole universe at one pinpoint Soul of all the universe. That which you manifest at your one pinpoint of the universe is remanifested in all of the universe. You cannot manifest separateness for there is no separateness to manifest.

You are divinity dwelling in the impenetrable dark of motion for long ages of seeking to penetrate the dark. You are the genius who has penetrated the dark to henceforth dwell in the Light. You are Conscious Mind, fully knowing the Light of your immortality, fully commanding your thinking and the body which images your thinking.

Let us now reconstruct the question to read: "Where does my body go when it dies?" The answer to that question is that your body does not die. It lies down to rest periodically for the purpose of renewal but its life and the body pattern, and the record of every thought you have ever given birth to, is enfolded in your Soul seed.

If you will but realize that your living body is but a machine which performs the work decreed for it to do by the Mind Intelligence which centers it, you will not have any concern about what happens to it. The only reason you have concern about your body is because of the long habit of thinking of your body as *you*.

Another thing which confuses you is that you think of your body as it is today. All you see of it is that part which is still living today, which weighs about 150 pounds. You never think of those parts of your body which are not living today. Every day of your whole life your body has been dying while you were constantly renewing it with more of your body than you took from the ground with which to renew it. You call it nourishment, but it is a constant renewal and repair process. That part of your body which has died has to be renewed with living tissue. That part of your machine which has worn out has to be repaired with new material.

One or two pounds of your body dies every day and is eliminated by its various processes. If you are seventy years old your body would weigh about twenty tons if parts of it had not died. Over nineteen and nine tenths of your body has already died. There are only one hundred and fifty pounds left of your body.

Why should you be more concerned about what happens to the few pounds of your body which are going to die, than you are concerned about the many tons of your body which have already died? The parts which have died have been returned to the ground. The small part which still remains should be returned to the ground in order that your new body and other bodies can be reborn from it.

Why should you be concerned about a few pounds of calcium, iron, manganese, iodine, nitrogen and other materials which built your body? They are not *you*. They are not your *identity*. They are the house you live in, but the house can burn down without affecting *you*. You can build another house to live in. That is what you do when your house of clay dissolves into its clay. *You* build another house of clay, another body. *You* are never without a body except during those periods of rest when you are repairing and replacing worn-out parts of your body, or building an entirely new one when the old one becomes too worn-out to renew or repair.

Let us look at it from this angle. It is a new angle of thought which should give you an entirely different idea of your body than the generally accepted one. Instead of thinking of your body as living and dying, think of your eternal Soul which is eternally living. Your Soul *extends* its life to your body to manifest the life which your Soul is. The body regives to the Soul that which has been extended to it. That is neither life nor death of the body. It is eternal life of the Soul expressed as two directions of life by the body.

You must, therefore, learn to think of life as action, and death as rest from action. Every day of your life is divided into action and rest from action. You are awake and active all day. Your body is thoroughly aware of its existence. But you rest each night and your body is as thoroughly unaware of its existence as though it were dead. The only reason you rest at night is to renew and repair your body. When your body is entirely worn-out you rest a longer time between periods of full renewal than between partial renewal. During those periods of acquiring an entirely new body, it is also unaware of bodily existence for a long period, instead of just one-night periods.

Nature tells the story of rebirth of bodies in very plain language. When you plant a seed in the ground for a flower, for a tree, or for a field of grass, these forms unfold from their seed into bodies. You think of these bodies as growing, dying and disappearing, but it almost escapes your notice that as every body unfolds from its seed it refolds back into it. For every branch and leaf of the oak tree you see with your eyes there is another branch and leaf which you do not see. What does that mean? It means that whatever unfolds from the seed to become a part of the visible universe, simultaneously refolds into its seed to disappear into the invisible universe. *The Soul does not wait to take your body back after it is all dead, it takes it back as fast as it gives it out.* There is your answer to what happens to your body when you die. Your Soul is your Self. *You* extend your body from your Soul-Self several billion times each second, and you return your body to your Soul-Self for rebirth at that same speed.

Everywhere in Nature you see rebirth of roses, of trees and of grass. Last year you picked an apple from this branch. This year you behold another apple where you plucked one last year, and the next year, and the next you can still pluck one. And if you open one you will find the same apple that you are going to eat all folded up in the seeds of other apples not yet born that will repeat the bodies of the apples which have long been born. That is Nature's eternal process of repeating eternal life. She divides eternal life into eternal repetitions of life. We call them life and death, but both of them are opposite expressions of life. Is not that a wonderful thing to know? Is it not wonderful to know that every day you live in the visible world of bodies, your every thought and action is also simultaneously repeated and recorded in the invisible world of Mind?

During all the ages of your unfolding as an individual entity you have repeated your own Self in each new body and every experience which has progressed or retarded you is also repeated. Whatever progress you now make in this life makes your next life expression easier for you. You continually advance as you learn new lessons.

You do not remember the nonessentials of each life, for that would be a terrible punishment. You would but live a life of continual remorse if you had to relive the experiences of the hard struggles which brought you out of the jungle into today's pleasant meadows. You do remember the essentials, however. If you have been a musician for several lives, and have thought music more than any other thought during those lives, you will undoubtedly think music again in succeeding lives. It is quite understandable why a musical prodigy exhibits such great musical talent at four or five years of age, if one thinks of it that way.

It is also quite understandable why some people are ahead of others and some so far behind. When you look over the human race you see many who exhibit the qualities of masters and leaders, while many more are but followers. That does not mean that some are "older Souls" than others, it simply means that some have made more of each life than others.

The great and wonderful thing about life is to learn to live it by profiting by every experience one must have on the long journey from body realization to Mind knowing, which also means from physical man to divine Spirit within man. The more you learn in each period of unfolding the more speedily you become aware of the kingdom of heaven within you as the goal of life. From that moment on the road is clear, for knowing the glory of life each period of it leads nearer and nearer to full illumination of Divine Consciousness in that Light.

SUMMARY

The first part of the journey of man from the dark of complete ignorance to the Light of Omniscience is entirely centered upon the import of his body. He knows naught else but body and requirements for body survival. His body works for him, fights for him, and provides him with its varying sensations and emotions.

After the dawn of Consciousness in him he acquires

knowledge which he thinks of as being a part of his body. He believes that his brain is that part of his body which thinks and knows. He builds a concept which links his identity and personal powers to his body. Together with that concept he thinks that body is reality and that all reality is limited to what the senses of the body can detect. This growing concept of early man gradually built up a reverence and concern for his body. When he died he thought that his identity died with him. His reverence for his dead self led him to build great tombs and sepulchers —even to such monuments for the dead as the great pyramids of Egypt.

As spiritual man unfolds, he gradually loses his sense of body reality until that great day of his awakening to Mind Consciousness when he loses all body reverence as full knowledge of its unreality dawns upon him. The highest moments of exaltation of the genius are those of complete forgetfulness of body. It must never be forgotten, however, that our bodies are marvelous instruments given to us to manifest our spiritual identity and as such should be revered and cared for as a means of expressing the beauty of God's Creation. The more we know how to care for it and keep it in balance with God's law, the more we can forget it to express Mind creativeness.

We are still in the early stages of human unfolding when we revere our dead bodies and have deep concern for them. Many still feel that their identities are buried with their bodies, and believe that "when you're dead you're dead." But practically all still ask, "Where do I go when I die?"

As the divinity of man awakens in him and he knows his Self as Mind which centers motion, his concern as to what happens to his body will wholly pass away from him.

That will be the great day of real knowing, the day when power in man is purely spiritual, the day when inner vision can see reality in the invisible CAUSE of the visible. This unfolding will some day come to man. He cannot avoid it, but the knowledge given herein will hasten its too slow unfolding by the hard way of paying for it through painful experience. It could save man many reincarnations by thus illumining his dark road with new Light.

PART III

*That which you do to others
you do to yourself.*
FACTUAL INTERPRETATION
OF THE GOLDEN RULE.

*Every action in Nature is simultaneously balanced
by an equal reaction.*
SCIENTIFIC INTERPRETATION
OF THE GOLDEN RULE.

*He who would command his destiny
must first learn how to balance
the conditions which control it.*
THE FIRST RULE OF LIFE.

LAO RUSSELL

CHAPTER XVI

Love Ye One Another

Love is the foundation of the world. All men are forever seeking it. They have forever been seeking it all
down the ages, but man is new. He does not yet know how
to find the love and happiness he seeks. He gropes for the
road to it, travels it a short way and plunges into an abyss.

The dawn has not yet come to help man see the road
and know how to find it. Once again he has traveled the
road of life a short way and is again falling into another
abyss of his own making. Man does not yet know how to
live with other men. *He has not yet found that every
other man on earth is a part of his very body, his very self,
not merely his brother.*

No man would intentionally hurt his own body but he
intentionally hurts other parts of his own body which he
thinks of as other men, not knowing that they are one
and inseparable from him. He knows that he cannot hurt
any part of his own body without hurting all of it, but he
has not yet found that he cannot hurt any man, anywhere,
without hurting himself and every man, everywhere. He
has only partly become aware that every happening anywhere, happens everywhere. Yes, he knows that, but he
thinks only of the human voice in that connection. The
radio is familiar to him. He hears the voice of the news
reporter telling of the anguish in Saigon, or Korea. He
also hears of the tortured in concentration camps, and of

hundreds of sons of the world-mother buried alive by their own other selves. They do not even know that they are also burying themselves and all mankind. Man does not yet know that the anguish of the homeless in Saigon is world anguish, not just for Saigon alone. Those homeless, barefoot mothers, carrying naked and hungry babies are not only walking from their burning homes into their own city, they are walking into your own doorway.

How many thousands of people in Europe have read of atrocities in other European countries, as you read of them here, and have thought, as you think, that "it could not happen here," only to find that it has happened there. We have comfortable homes, a car and every necessity of life. So had they, but there were those who "know not what they do," who stepped into factories and homes and ordered them out with nothing but the clothing on their backs.

Three thousand miles away means nothing. What happens three thousand miles away happens in our own homes. People who are hurt three thousand miles away are being hurt in our own homes, for what happens anywhere happens everywhere. Thousands of our own sons died while the people of Korea, nine thousand miles away, were being hurt. Their hurt was every man's hurt. When one part of the world is suffering untold agonies and our part of the world boasts of great and increasing prosperity, as we are now doing, we are living in a fool's paradise. Those untold sufferings of the other half of the world are debits which must be deducted from our credits to make us poorer each year instead of richer. No country can call itself "richer" when it profits itself by another nation's poverty. Our riches of today are the fruits of world crime. They always have been. This has always been a gangster world which enriches itself by impoverishing others. No gangster has ever been able to hold what he has stolen and live in peace, without having armored cars and body-guards to help him try to hold it. For such a man to call himself rich, prosperous, and happy because of his mighty possessions, is living in the fool's paradise that our world is living in. Never in history has this man-made gangster world ever had to have so many armored cars, and so huge a bodyguard, to protect itself and its mighty possessions from further confiscation by greater gangsters.

Only one decade ago we ended a second war which we had fought to end wars. We looked for an era of peace, but instead of that we have spent many more billions to protect ourselves from more enemies that our unbalanced civilization has been perpetually making for ages. Shall we again have to fight another war to end wars? If so, will it end them? Has war ever ended in peace and happiness without leaving an accumulation of fear, hatred and enmity to breed more wars?

Yes—we know that it is necessary—and expedient—but what kind of world is it that makes such an expedient become a necessity? Where is the wisdom of building that kind of world by people whose sole desire in life is to find happiness, peace and prosperity? "Man always kills the thing he loves," and that is what he has done again and what he must pay for. The game of seesaw, which life is, cannot be played very long with a full-grown man on one end of it and a little girl on the other end. Nor can our civilization continue the game for very long with an elephant on one end and an ant on the other, as it is so hysterically trying to do.

Again I say that the only hope for saving this unhappy, unbalanced world of fear is to start all over again and make a new world which has in it the aggressive and force-ful character of the male, equally balanced by the restrain-ing spiritual force which directs the male force into *con-structive,* instead of *destructive* directions. We may as well do this *now,* instead of continuing in the old self-suicidal way, for Natural law will not permit such unbalance to continue.

It is time that we looked at the falsity of the riches we boast about and realize that our country is poorer today than it has ever been in history. This once bountifully solvent nation is insolvent today. Its debts are greater than the real estate values of the whole country. Every child who has been born since 1950 is many thousands of dollars in debt at birth, with no assets to pay that debt, and no hope of getting out of debt during his whole life. Not one man in this country owns his own home, because it is first security for a national debt, thus making every citizen in-solvent. That is why our so-called prosperity has no foun-dation, for we have made our nation prosperous by mak-ing its people insolvent.

Do not, therefore, say that "it cannot happen here," when it has already happened here. Do not also say that we are rich and prosperous because everyone is earning money by taking it from his own pocket to fill another pocket of his own. Do not be so sure for even what you think you have may not be yours tomorrow.

When the world talks prosperity because we have sold a million more automobiles this year than last, and the stock market is higher than ever before in history, that is but one side of the world ledger. The other side of the world ledger, however, tells us that there is a correspond-ing increase in crimes, criminals and youth delinquents. Also that there are billions and billions being spent to protect us from our enemies in order that we may even survive to do business. Thousands of American lives are being sacrificed to protect us from enemies which we made by business greed.

These tragic items are our fixed overhead charges which enable us to build our seeming prosperity. Where then are the profits?

What people fail to realize is that seeming world prosperity will not save a falling civilization. The Babylonian, Greek and Roman civilizations were luxuriously wealthy when they fell. Too much luxury even contributed to the fall of civilizations just as money and luxury in a home often degenerate progressive families into what are known as the idle rich.

Moral degeneracy alone destroys civilizations. Money or prosperity is not a controlling factor. Even if we sell fifty million more cars this year than last, or even if stocks sell for five times as much this year than last, this civilization will as surely fall as other morally decadent civilizations fall unless the *cause* of its falling is removed. One might as consistently tell a man who has a very bad heart that nothing can happen to him because his business is doubling its profits yearly.

Why is all this? We do not know how to live. We place money values even ahead of life itself. We do not know the value of our neighbor to ourselves. We do not even know the relationship of our neighbor to ourselves. We have no living philosophy to live by, we have but a philosophy to die by. That philosophy is based upon disunity, separateness and greed. That is what I mean by the philosophy of death. It means that you cannot live by it. *A living philosophy must be based upon unity—oneness —inseparability and interdependence.* It must have *love* as its motive instead of *fear*. It must see the good in man and not look upon him as sinful and evil. *The world becomes what the world thinks*. It thinks of man as sinful and evil and he has become what his own thoughts have made him. He has made a world of hate and fear, and where hate is love cannot also be.

There will come a time, however, when the whole human race will know itself as one family, with but the one FATHER-MOTHER of all. When that day comes every man will be the father and mother, or brother and sister, or son and daughter of every other man. As love comes into the world with spiritual unfolding, separateness and disunity go out of it. With love comes knowledge of the power of unity which makes the power of every man become the power of every other man. Separateness and selfishness breed each other. Separateness makes one man want for himself what every other man also wants for himself. Separateness takes. It never gives, and long ages of taking must pass before he learns that *what he takes he never has, but what he gives he always has*.

The long ages will pass, however, and every man will serve every other man whom he knows as his very Self. Blood relationship is mighty in its desire to serve sons and daughters, or brothers and sisters, and fathers and mothers in one separate family. No matter what wrong a son may do to the whole world, the love of parents is greater than the fault.

The happy, peaceful and progressive home is one where each member of the family thinks first of each other member, serves *first* each other before himself, and freely gives without motive of self-gain. In the ideal family everyone will not only serve each other to make him happy but will refrain from doing anything to make any member of it unhappy. That is the ideal. That is what every home needs to make complete happiness for every member of it.

The world is one family of one world-home. The ideal world is one in which every member of it serves each other lovingly to give him happiness, and refrains from doing anything which will take his happiness away from him. That is the ultimate goal. That is what mankind is striving for. That is what he has been striving for over the long aeons. For these long ages he has ever been searching for the road which will lead to that goal of romance and peace.

Yes—that is the ideal—and the goal—but how very far the world-family is from such a goal! And how far the average individual family is away from it. It would be difficult to find such a family anywhere, but there are many of them who have so nearly approached it that their example is a light shining out of the darkness.

As for the world-family, that ideal is still so far away that it may again destroy itself several times before it learns its lesson sufficiently to function as a whole. If you know any family in your town whose members are as divided against each other as our present world-family, you know for a certainty that such a family will break apart and go to pieces. You would know that its disunity would destroy it eventually. It would seem that the world-family has not even found the road which leads to unity and cohesiveness as yet.

Oh, how many individuals and families have thought that they had found the road to happiness and have lost it in just not knowing how to live it. We have never really known how to live life, either individually, or collectively, as families, cities and nations. Life is an experiment in trying to find a way of life. It is full of the comedies, tragedies and other problems which confront everyone all of the time. They are always here, in your home and mine, in your life and mine. And the greatest problem is *how to meet them and dissolve them.*

That is what I want to talk over with you for the rest of this book. To have a living philosophy which will meet all problems alike and rise above them with glory, rather than anguish, and become strong because of them, is of first import in man's self-education. Problems are all alike in principle. They differ only in details and form, like the ten thousand stories written around the same motive, so let us take a familiar one which thousands of men and women are facing in this immature civilization which is, as yet, but coming out of the dark.

A very happy woman was sure she had found romance, love, peace and security. Then one day her whole world crumbled and fell at her feet. Her husband telephoned her that he would be detained at the office until late. He had telephoned her a hundred times before saying he would be detained and she had never known a moment's concern, for she had known in her heart that it was all right. This time it was different. She trembled with some dread fear, even before lifting the receiver. His voice was the same cheerful voice but there was something strangely different about it. She was deeply disturbed, for some bits of gossip had reached her ears which she had ignored, but intuition was making it difficult to answer with the naturalness of her own cheerful voice.

For a long time she sat in silence by the telephone after hanging up the receiver. Something which had never entered that home before came into it at that moment. That which entered her home that night was the dread destroyer of all that man calls good in man's world. Its name is *tension.* Tension came into her home, her heart and her romance, to multiply until happiness became impossible for one who did not know how to meet it in any other way than tears, weepings, supplications and compromise.

When such a tragedy threatens the happiness of any woman or man, the event itself is of far less importance than the way one meets it. How will this particular woman meet it? That is what is important. As we are seeking a right way of life, and as life is full of big and little problems, let us take this particular problem of this grief-stricken woman and discuss the merits and philosophy from the point of view of Natural law and God's ways and processes.

There are two ways of meeting every problem of life. This grief-stricken woman has her choice of those two ways. One way is the way of weakness, of tears, grief, pleadings and supplications. *That is the wrong way. It multiplies tensions by compromising. It attempts to cure wrong with wrong.* That is the weak way which creates a long life of continuous unhappiness. The strong way is by not compromising and knowing how to intelligently meet such a challenge. The weak way begins with multiplying tensions instead of dissolving them. That is the first thing that anyone should think of in meeting any problem. Whatever tension has been created by the appearance of that problem must be dissolved. It must be utterly eliminated, no matter what price must be paid in humility and material loss. Tensions cannot exist in anyone's life without his permission, nor without nourishment supplied by him. *Happiness and tension cannot possibly co-exist.*

A few agonizing weeks pass and this woman, whom we will call Sarah, has become quite convinced that another woman has come between herself and her husband. Being no longer able to stand the grief of it alone she takes her first wrong step. Instead of working in the direction of dissolving the existent tension, Sarah tells her mother all about it. There are tears and much grief. Her mother is sorrowful and sympathetic. She shares her daughter's trouble with her. They cry a little together. Sarah thinks she feels a little better by feeling her mother's love and sympathy but what has really happened is that Sarah has created another tension and another problem.

Tensions cannot create happiness, they destroy it. Unintentionally Sarah took happiness away from her mother for herself but found only an increased tension and another problem. Two people now have a tension instead of one and the problem is doubled by the fact that the mother will either do something about it herself or advise Sarah to do something which Sarah should not do.

Weak people always seek the advice of others. Strong people never do. Strong people may seek information but their decisions are their own. We tell our students that the only one to ever ask advice from is God. When you have a decision to make, go into your place of quiet, in your own room or out in the woods, or down by the sea, anywhere, where you can be all alone with God. He will *always* give you the *right* answer. *You already have the right answer within you.* God will but *awaken* you to a realization of that fact. Talk to God as you would talk to one you know whom you can love and trust beyond all others.

That is what Sarah should have done instead of complexing her problem by going to her mother. One cannot shift one's mental burden to another for each man's problem is his alone. When the burden of Sarah's problem was given to her mother, instead of facing and solving it her-self, the problem had doubled itself. Two now had it in-stead of one. Soon four had it, for Sarah's mother told Sarah's father and he consulted a lawyer. They all talked, and the town heard of it, and the gossips spread it. By the time Sarah had decided to talk to her husband, he had de-cided that the only right thing he could do was to get a divorce.

The happy ending, which could have been possible, was rendered impossible by the mere multiplication of one tension into a hundred. What he might have said to her alone, where he could open his heart to her, might have cured her heartache and saved their home. They could have both counted it as one of those human experi-ences that all people at some time encounter in their lives, which enrich one's life if conquered, but impoverish it if the experience is the conqueror.

When Sarah talked with her husband her mother was with her to protest, to condemn and blame, and her father and lawyer were there to build an impenetrable wall around the case to keep peace and happiness out of it. Love knocked hard on the doors of that wall in the hope of being allowed to come in where the light of his love could be seen in his eyes, and felt in their hearts. The words of the mother locked the doors still tighter and the formality of the father and lawyer made love stop knock-ing at the door to weep instead.

Thus it was that one more home was broken up. A problem of life—just one of the thousands of problems of life which will forever confront you, and me, and every-one who lives, succeeded in becoming real, instead of its unreality being dissolved as black clouds dissolve to let the light come through.

That is what came of meeting that problem the wrong way, the weak way of self-injury, the way of tears, and grief, and a bid for sympathy, compassion and pity.

Had Sarah been a very strong woman and met her problem the way it should have been met from the first moment that she became aware of it, the very first thing she would do would be to dissolve that mental tension which the shock of discovery caused in her. The strong person is one who learns to take all things alike without affecting that inner ecstasy for long, which gives one strength. That high state of happiness is the spiritual in one which so far transcends any human emotions that nothing can touch one beyond a passing moment. Such a person can find balance speedily, no matter what tension comes into his life to disturb its balance.

I know a strong man whose heart was so full of the rhythms of the singing of all Nature that he was able to continue the farce of matrimony, in name-only existence, for many many years, as mere background for his picture of life. He could at all times walk away into the woods with a biscuit in his pocket and spend a day in ecstasy of Mind. His sketchbook recorded the beauty of motives for nocturnes and symphonies, or perhaps the graceful branches and great tree trunks which held them up into the high heavens, told of his all-day loving communion with them and their Creator. He thus immunized himself from even the possibility of a disturbing tension.

When serious tensions arise between man and wife they should first talk to God about them. A natural state of happiness must first be restored. When one talks to God about any trouble on the waters of life they become calm and still, and one who knows the ecstasy of the kingdom of heaven within one's Self finds that heaven, and knows that nothing on earth can hurt one unless one accepts the hurt. Good thoughts dissolve unpleasant ones.

When calm has been restored, then is the time to sit down quietly together and face the cause of the original tension. From such a discussion both parties will often discover that both have unknowingly contributed to the rift. Perhaps either one, or the other, has felt a lack of romance and sought it from another. When these marital differences are faced together alone—without multiplying tensions by outside advice and interferences—they can usually be dissolved and good can come from them. There are very few who can possibly pass through life without having experiences which they deeply regret, but with knowledge they can strengthen their character and immunize themselves from a repetition of the same or more serious ones. *Thus good can come from an experience which could also destroy one.*

People in all the world forever seek love, but few find it, for very few know where to seek it or how to find it. And many shut it out from themselves because the love they seek must fit within a motive, or pattern, which they have created for the use of love. He who seeks love with a personal motive behind it will never find it. If money, or personal support, or social position is the motive they may find what they seek but they will not have found love. Like the man who seeks happiness through money, he may find the money but not the happiness he sought.

Love can have but one motive, to give out from itself in order to find unity. The greatest urge in all Nature is UNITY.

This quality in Nature is so little understood, and so rarely practiced as a consequence, that it must be dwelt upon and made clear. Unity means the ending of separate-

ness, of division or multiplication, or difference of opinion, or anything whatsoever which can be said to be two.
Unity means complete ONENESS.

Separateness is in itself the quality of tension. Every
state of motion in the universe is exerted either for creating tensions or eliminating them. A man who deeply
desires money must use much effort to obtain it. That effort creates a tension. When he has obtained all he wants
and locks it up to keep it for himself, he does not realize
that he has locked up the tension of accumulating it. He
no longer has the money he sought for the purpose of giving him happiness. He has but the tension of worry and
strain of keeping it. He must watch it lest thieves take it
from him.

To thus lock one's happiness in a box, as Scrooge did,
means that he is without happiness, as Scrooge was. The
moment he gives love and happiness out to one who
needs it, love and happiness will be regiven to him. He
then has what he has given, but never can have while it is
locked in a box for himself alone.

Even this example must be amplified, for very many
people do not understand what Jesus meant when he told
the rich man to go and sell all he had and give it to the
poor.

I once heard a rich man combat that idea severely. He
argued that if he sold all he had and gave a million dollars
to the poor he would himself be poor, and those to whom
he gave his million would also be as poor the next day.

That would be only giving money to people who
wanted only money and had no way of regiving money,
I explained, but if you gave love with the money by giving it out of yourself, they would then have a way of regiving both the love and the money. In such a way of

giving you never could be poor for you could never give it without a balancing regiving.

Suppose that there were five hundred poor and needy families in your town. Instead of dividing your million dollars with them in money you bought a textile industry and divided that up with them to give permanent employment to all of them. They would then have the happiness of permanent security which they would regive to you in love. And you would have the happiness of giving them the love which they needed. And the million dollars would soon be two million which they also would regive to you.

That is what Jesus meant when He said "all you have." He did not mean money alone. He also meant the love you had in you to give which money made possible, but the love was not in the money, it was in the man. The money without the love is worthless.

When a man thus gives himself "to the poor," as well as giving his money, he finds unity through action, which Nature demands to complete her transactions. Otherwise, he would merely have been giving only charity which is not in conformity with Nature's law. Nature demands that everything given be equally regiven.

Self-created tensions which destroy the happiness of many families have numerous illustrations in homes where mothers and fathers prevent their children from living normal lives by insisting upon living their lives for them.

A very happy home of father, mother, a daughter and son lived together in great harmony until both children became old enough to court, and be courted. The father died and the mother suddenly developed the idea that her children should sacrifice their lives for her. Instead of the natural desire of wanting to see her children happily married the thought of losing them struck terror in her heart. Since losing her husband she felt that their sole purpose henceforth was to take their father's place in her affections and support. She had to fall back on her old occupation of dressmaking to support them until both children were able to work and support her.

Tensions began when Susan's first beau came to spend an evening with her in her home. Her mother strongly resented this first serious threat to her happiness. Susan was told that she was not old enough to think of such things. She also had her mother to consider and could not waste time on boys. The mother sat through the young man's first visit, and the second, but a third visit did not take place. The boy sought other and more pleasant fields. Love had not ripened in him far enough to make a fight for love against such resistance. Young love must have suitable soil to grow in just as a young plant must also have suitable soil to grow in.

Dick also spent evenings with different girls and went to many parties, but when he seemed to prefer one certain girl his mother reminded him that he was not to think of such things while she needed his love and support. She so imbued both children with that idea that they gradually came to believe it. Year by year went by in this same manner. Each of them felt their mother's possessiveness. She constantly reminded them of her years of self-sacrifice—years she had given for them—and of their first duty to their mother. From the moment that the mother's assertion of possession of her children began, happiness flew out of the window of that home. The first tension began at that moment. As tension multiplied its potential, happiness divided it. When tensions grow strong enough in families, something snaps.

Susan had grown to be thirty-four and Dick thirty-six. Susan had been put on the hopeless list by suitors for a long time. She had received hardly any attention for years. Then something happened. A boy whom she deeply loved and wanted to marry when she was twenty-six, who had left at that time to take a position in another town, returned home. A great surge of suppressed happiness came to Susan followed by a deeper surge of tears when she thought of her duty to her mother, which had been so indelibly instilled in her. Her suitor would not take "No" for an answer, saying: "Your mother has already taken ten years of happiness away from us. She is an unnatural mother and I shall tell her so. You can contribute your share to her support, as usual, but you are going to marry me and that's the end of that."

There was a scene, a memorable scene, but something snapped in Dick, too, and he said things to his mother that he never dreamed possible, so hypnotized had he been by the idea that sacrifice for his mother was his unquestionable duty. When he found that the assurance of continued support meant so little to her in comparison with the desire to possess her children, he said to her: "Mother, you have had your marital happiness, you have had a husband and children and a home. It is not you who have sacrificed for us. You have sacrificed us for you. Susan loves John and should have married him ten years ago. She will marry him now and I will marry Nancy who is growing old waiting for me. You should find happiness in your added children and grandchildren, as other mothers do. I hope you will too, but we have finally awakened to the truth of the situation and shall live our normal lives as you lived yours."

This particular mother was unable to adjust herself to the naturalness of family growth because she had never learned to give happiness by sharing. She was unable to find happiness in the midst of an abundance of it. Therefore, she manufactured her own loneliness and unhappiness. Thus one more home in which were all the elements for making happiness was broken up by not knowing how to live life in harmony with the one law of balance which governs all life. This was just one more problem of the many thousands of problems which everyone meets continuously. There should be no difficulty in meeting any one of them if people have unfolded far enough spiritually to first ask God to tell them how to settle their problems.

The law courts are jammed with thousands of human problems which need not be there. Every man who sues another man knows in his heart what is the right thing for him to do, and the man who is sued also knows what is the right thing for him to do. Both knowing that, and knowing that the right way is the only way, why do they still fight each other in court, like enemies, instead of sitting down together as friends? The answer is that the majority of people who go to law with their economic difficulties either want to get the best of the other fellow and get all they can for themselves or dodge a responsibility which they know they should meet. By defending an action they hope to dodge much more of that responsibility than by paying it in full.

One of our lawyer students said that fully seventy percent of our economic problems could be settled out of court if people really wanted to be fair. He has caused many of his clients to sit face to face with their opponents and settle their differences on a fair basis, which keeps friendships, instead of on a forced basis, which loses friendships. He cited a case where his client's opponent refused to meet in a friendly way to discuss a suit for heavy damages, which his opponent insisted upon instituting. This lawyer and his client had concluded that a generously fair amount due to the opponent was fifty thousand dollars and had offered that amount in a friendly communication.

The offer was refused and the suit for $200,000 went into court which awarded only $20,000 instead of $200,000 on the ground of contributory negligence on the part of the plaintiff. When the client said to his attorney: "Well, John, we have saved $30,000 by his going to law," the attorney surprised him by replying: "No, we have not saved $30,000 for we are going to send him the $50,000 which we offered him."

"Why in the world do we do that? We won the case did we not?" the client asked. "Yes, we won it but we will lose it if we do not do what we thought in our hearts was fair to do. If the law gives him less than what we thought fair we are hurting ourselves by taking advantage of it and losing a friend as well."

A check for $50,000 was sent with a letter which started with these words: "Dear John: I deeply regret the decision of the court in the case just settled. We may have disagreed between ourselves about the amount you were entitled to and that we should pay, but our conclusion that we fairly owed you the amount of our enclosed check cannot be altered by even a court decision, which we are unwilling to accept as fair."

It is needless to say that such a conclusion canceled out a tension which might never have been canceled out in the lifetime of those two men. Had the check for $20,000 been sent to the plaintiff's attorney through the attorney for the defendant, there would be a residual tension accompanying that check which might have cost ten times the $30,000 saved in good will.

The combativeness of human nature disappears entirely when the love force of Nature destroys separateness and its consequent selfishness. Combativeness and selfish desires of getting all that one can out of a transaction with another man is an attempt to bargain with God. That is impossible. God will not let you take more than the law or less than the law. If you force a settlement with your neighbor for less than Nature's one law of balance should give you, there will come with it a costly tension which can never be canceled.

To better comprehend the permanent damage of a tension which always lasts until canceled, take a strong piece of rubber and stretch it as far as you can and hold it there. Not for one second can you be unaware of that straining tension which you have made for yourself. If you were obliged to hold it in that position you would give all you had to be freed from it. Try also to do your daily tasks while leaning even three degrees from your equally balanced position. Just that little three degrees would make your life many times more difficult and uncomfortable, yet practically every man on earth is in that position, or worse.

Every man has a certain number of tensions that he has created in his daily life which he must continually work against. Added to that is a great world tension of unknown power which everyone knows could destroy half the world overnight. That great world tension exists. No one knows exactly what it is but everyone feels an ominous threat of an unknown something in the air which prevents complete happiness. Wherever tensions exist anywhere complete happiness is impossible. That is why every problem which comes into anyone's life should be faced immediately, no matter what it is, and eliminated. Search for the *cause* of it. You probably made it in some dealing during the day. If you are disturbed about it that means that there is a residual unbalance in it that you have not canceled. You cannot possibly be completely happy until you have voided that residual unbalance. It is as though it is making you lean several degrees off center from gravity.

A renowned New York industrialist, who attributes his success to fair dealing and giving service instead of taking it, said that if he found that he had hurt a friend he would seek him out at once and heal his hurt before the day could pass. That is such a simple principle to understand that it is strange that people do not realize it. Many a marriage could be saved if before going to sleep either the husband or wife said "I love you," after there had been a discordant note which left even a slight tension.

Consider the common problem of loneliness in a world where everyone is seeking friendships. Every lonely person is surrounded by love and friendship which is hers, or his, for the asking. They want to take it in instead of giving it out. They want attention to be shown to them instead of giving service to others. They wait for it to be given to them without giving anything out to others. Everyone who wants love and companionship can have it in abundance if they will only give loving friendship to everyone they meet. One cannot keep love away from one's self if one gives love. The girl who radiates friendliness and charm of manner attracts many more friends than the haughty self-centered one who demands admiration for herself.

Lao-tzu once said: "He who desires honors should first

honor others." One who desires admiration must, therefore, first give admiration, or forever be without it.

It matters not what your trouble or problem may be if
you will but realize that God has forever whispered His
loving instructions to you since your very beginning. God
works with all of His creations all of the time. When,
after long ages, men become aware of it, their very destinies are simplified by learning how to work with Him.
Do not, therefore, wait until you go to bed to make your
habitual prayer to Him. Be aware of His presence within
you every moment, so that you are as aware that He is
working with you as you are aware that your partner is
working with you.

Moment to moment awareness of God's presence is
needed for unfolding your destiny through work, and it
is also needed to retain a state of perpetual inner joyousness which will immunize you from the toxins of fatigue.
Joyousness is love. One whose nature is joyous will very
often not show the slightest signs of fatigue, while the
morose one, or one who does not love the work he is doing, will fatigue very quickly.

Again I say, life is difficult to live when one does not
know the kingdom of heaven which centers him. The
more that anyone acquires conscious awareness of God's
eternal presence within him, the easier the living of life
becomes.

This chapter closes with the admonishment to "Love
Ye One Another," as it opened with those same words,
and as every chapter of life's experiences should begin
and end, for Love is the foundation of Life.

CHAPTER XVII

Character

If you could see a sculptor at work upon a head you would be fascinated with the gradual appearance of character from a characterless mass of clay. Gradually the eyes, nose and mouth begin to shape themselves into the strong features of a well-known statesman. It would amaze you at some stages of the work to see a tiny change in the line of the mouth, or the upturn at its corners, or just a little more clear-cut firmness given to it. A slight touch here and there in the forehead and cheeks, and especially the eyes, and the strength of a great character emerges from the shapeless clay.

Perhaps you may not realize that you are sculpturing your own features that way. You started as a baby with a perfectly characterless face and body. What you look like today is what you have sculptured the clay of your body to become. If there is firmness and strength of great character there you have been the sculptor of it. If there is weakness and vacillation there you also modeled that into your features. All men and women sculpture themselves in their own image.

Perhaps you have not thought of that. Most people, who do not give much thought to it, vaguely imagine that they are created to look as they look. They think that they just grew that way. That is not right thinking. Everyone looks different because he has a different type of body,

but the character and expression are different only because people think differently.

From the moment you are born your own human nature and your own character begin to impress your individuality upon your whole body. Every thought you
think is just like one movement of the sculptor's fingers
upon his clay, which turns the corners of your mouth up,
or down, to depict a cheerful person or an ugly one.

Children have very little character in their faces because they have not lived long enough to have had sufficient experiences in their lives to make character. Even
at an early age, however, you can tell what kind of character the grown-up child will be by what he thinks and
does. If I see a boy spending hour after hour looking at
television, or keeping the radio turned on all the time, I
know what he will look like when he grows up. He will
not be bright looking, nor keen and intelligent, for he
wants to be entertained all the time from sources outside
of himself. Even though he does look at television quite a
little, one boy will choose programs which have something of a cultural value, while another boy would turn
these off and choose the sensational programs.

If your children are inventive and have imagination
they will spend their time in making things instead of forever seeking to be amused from sources outside of themselves.

Boys or girls of ten have strong beginnings of character,
but they are only the beginnings. Up to fourteen years of
age your children are most pliable. You can help them to
model their own characters better before, than after that
age. "As the twig is bent so is the tree inclined." After
fourteen the wood of the tree is too firm for easy bending.
Also if you see boys or girls who are very busy all the time

doing something, making little cakes and dolls, or kites and toy planes, you know that they will be more resourceful and self-sufficient when they grow up than the boys or girls who never know what to do and want to be taken somewhere, or to be shown what to do. That amount of character is already modeled into their features by themselves.

You must not make the mistake of judging all children alike, however. There are the dreamers who think inwardly and find a sufficiency within themselves. These are often mistaken for subnormal children, when, in fact, they are the reverse. The reason they may not be so active of body is because they are active of Mind. They have keen imaginations and are never so happy as when they are left alone with their own imaginings. When you see such qualities in children you may well count upon it that they would make poor business executives but would be excellent creators in the fine arts or designing professions. Many such children suffer untold agony because of not being understood by their families.

Every young girl wants to look beautiful. How many thousands of times every teen-age girl looks in the mirror and wishes she was as beautiful as some other girl she knows. The way to look beautiful is to have beautiful thoughts. No one can help being beautiful if one thinks beautiful thoughts, and no one can prevent himself from looking ugly if he has ugly thoughts. Have you ever seen a Sister of Mercy, or a nun, who is not beautiful? No matter what her features are she is always beautiful. Nuns lives are dedicated to giving loving service to others. Love is modeled into their every feature. They cannot help becoming the image of their own thinking.

I remember when I was about seventeen. Girls of my

age dreaded growing old. Usually they considered a woman of forty as being very old. I would silently watch the woman of thirty-five and forty, or more, and think how beautiful and poised she was and think how wonderful it would be when I reached thirty-five. I have always thought of young girls as pretty, mature women as beautiful and old ladies as lovely.

Pretty young girls have not had the necessary emotions of life as yet to make them beautiful, for beauty is not just in form alone. Beauty is dependent entirely upon how much love a woman has put into her thinking. A woman may have a face as pretty as a doll and be repellent if she has led a selfish or cynical life. I have seen many doll-like beautiful women who had deceit and treachery written into every line in their faces. On the other hand I have seen very plain women who were supremely beautiful because of the love they gave to the world. Love is the greatest sculptor of beauty. Florence Nightingale gave love from out of her saintly nature for many years. She was not a beautiful woman in feature, as the world judges beautiful women, but her countenance was luminous with a Madonna Light which inspired one who was fortunate enough to be uplifted by it.

I remember a woman of about forty who was in our choir when I was a young girl. She had prematurely white hair which came to her suddenly because of a great sorrow. Everyone in the audience looked at her with much more interest than at any of the young girls. They did that for there was more of the character of beauty in her face than in the younger characterless faces, and her beautiful white hair was truly her crowning glory.

Naturally the same principles which apply to women in age and appearance also apply to men. Personally I have always thought that the older a man grows the more handsome he becomes. For verification of this look over some old photographs of men you know. Even though they may have the handicap of losing all of their hair, they still look much more handsome than as young men with shocks of curly hair.

My husband became the world's most famous painter of children. Almost overnight he found that he could no longer continue to paint them for he craved to express the great beauty of older people who had lived useful, creative lives. Everyone wondered why he could possibly do such a thing as to give up painting beautiful, innocent young opening buds of life, after he had so masterfully conquered the subtleties demanded by such subjects. His answer was that he tired of painting maps upon which the emotions of a lifetime are going to be impressed. They ceased to inspire him. He craved painting faces upon which the emotions of a lifetime had been impressed, instead of the blankness of mere prettiness. He once said that there is more inspiring beauty in the face of an old wrinkled peasant woman, who has mothered seven children under great difficulties, than there is in the most beautiful woman in the world, who has lived for herself alone.

What character is there in the calm ocean as compared with the tempest tossed waters of roaring winds and crashing waves on rockbound shores? What opportunity for character is there in the face of the insulated office clerk as compared with the explorer of African or Brazilian jungles? We can, perhaps, say that the face of a gently bred man, whose background is the drawing room of social life, is more handsome, but, is it more interesting?

I often recall Barrie, the famous English playwright,

saying that a plain woman with charm is more beautiful and attractive than a beautiful woman who is without charm. Why is that? Charm comes from giving love out of one's self to others. It lies in consideration and thoughtfulness shown to others, and more especially in cheerfulness of disposition which uplifts everyone with whom a person of charm comes in contact.

I know of a woman who had great charm when she was with her close friends and immediate family. She seemed to lose it completely when she was with strangers. This worried her very much for she was always the wallflower at parties, had great difficulty with dinner partners who ignored her and talked to their companions on the other side. She gradually developed a strong inferiority complex because of it, even though she was very beautiful, not yet thirty and a musician of repute.

One day she confided her troubles to me and I told her that all of her troubles were the effects of one simple fault. I said, "you are afraid of people, especially men." "That is nonsense, I love to be with all people, men and women. I am not at all afraid of them," she replied. "If you are not afraid of them why do you draw slightly back when you are introduced to any stranger?" I asked. "There is no more repelling gesture in the lexicon of how to be friends with anyone than that. You have a most chilling reserve with all strangers. I noticed it when you were introduced to our guests. If you would just reverse that attitude and lean forward when you are greeting others who lean forward to greet you, your troubles would end that instant. Try it," I said.

She did try it, and very conscientiously. Hardly a week passed before she felt a great difference in her life. She no longer had any difficulty in holding her dinner partners when she leaned just a little toward them in the natural way of friends, instead of always drawing back, even ever so slightly. Very soon she had admirers and boxes of flowers. Soon she married a very prominent man. When we last heard of her she said that the most important thing she was trying to give to her children was charm.

The greatest mistake one who is growing old can make is to dread it, and try to evade it, by any artificial means whatsoever, beyond those which good care demands. White hair is beautiful when the time comes for white hair. To dye white hair black or red, as countless women do, is to rob themselves of the character and charm which makes old age so lovely and interesting. Instead of improving one, it has the opposite effect of making one look as artificial as the lily would be if one painted it. Probably the greatest crime in this respect is to "lift one's face" by a surgical operation. All too frequently one looks positively grotesque who has thus tried to reverse the effects of time by taking all the glory and wonder away from her face.

A well-known woman in musical circles had raven black hair which won her so many compliments that she felt her world was coming to an end when white hairs first appeared in that beautiful blackness. To delay it even a little, she dyed those few white hairs, but she could never stop dying them as they increased in number. It was not noticeable for years, but it became very noticeable, and then conspicuously so. She could not bear to allow herself to change, however, even though she ceased to hear the compliments which gave her such pleasure in her earlier years. When she passed well into her seventies she had an illness which kept her in a hospital for months, and still more months for convalescing. During that period her hair became its natural snow-white and she then again received many compliments for the loveliness of her hair. She had not realized that she was working against Nature which was trying to keep her always beautiful and she was preventing Nature from doing that.

Another interesting story I remember in connection with growing older is one about a woman whose sweetheart of twenty years before, who was then financially unable to marry her, wrote that he was now returning as a wealthy man. In the meantime, she had been unhappily married and the experience had sculptured its lines on her face and her once blond hair was streaked with white. Her first thought upon receiving his letter was that he would be shocked when he saw her for he would be thinking of her as she was twenty years ago. She decided she must dye her hair blond again and have her face lifted to get rid of the aging lines.

He telephoned her from the station when he arrived and the joy that they both felt told its own story. Her heart beat fast as she opened the door to let him in. There stood a fine looking middle-aged man with hair graying at the temples and with that warmth of naturalness that comes with age. He looked hard into her face and with a growing look of incredulity said, "Why Elizabeth, you have not changed at all." The mature romance he had returned to find had somehow disappeared, for this young-looking woman was not what he wanted *now*—he wanted a mature woman who could share all things with him. Life had not touched this woman and he felt she would not be able to give him the richness of the love he sought.

The lesson of this story is that as people grow old they

forget that all of their friends also grow old with them. When one of them tries to look younger by artificial means, the naturalness of growth and friendship is strained. When one grows old gracefully, with Nature and time, Nature always works with them to sculpture whatever character they have become into their bodies.

The idea of import which lies back of this idea is that everyone has become the image of his own thinking. He may not have become what he wants to be because he may not have been willing to put forth the effort of becoming what he wants to be. In that case you see other characteristics in his features. You see frustration, weakness, vacillation and laziness there. You do not see in such a face the strength of a man who will go out to get what he wants with love for the very effort of it.

The world is so full of people who have tremendous desires which they wish to obtain by wishful thinking, or by having someone else make it easy for them. Such people who desire to become great characters can become great characters by making the necessary effort. That is the only way anyone can become great. Desire alone is not sufficient.

I often think of a woman who is now a well-known writer who started her career as a stenographer but desired more than anything else to write good fictional stories for adaptation for movies. Every evening, and way into the night, she wrote her stories. Finally one was accepted by a leading magazine. That was her beginning, but it still meant months, perhaps years, of giving every evening to her writing. She had the strength of character necessary for achievement and eventually wrote a fine story that she sold to another leading magazine, and for which she also received $50,000 for the film rights.

How many people say they could write fine stories if they only had the time or the money to study. This woman had neither but she had an indomitable desire and belief in herself that nothing could quench. Only sheer hard work brought fruition to her desires.

The personnel director of any great industry becomes very proficient in judging the character into which people sculpture themselves. One young man, freshly graduated from school, was shown into the director's room. Instead of waiting for the first question to come from the director, he said: "I am answering your advertisement for men. What are the hours and what do you pay?" "Young man, I am afraid you have very much to learn in life but we have no time to teach it to you here," the director replied as he asked his secretary to show the next applicant in.

A good personnel man can look over fifty applicants without personally interviewing any of them and eliminate two thirds of them without taking time for interviews. Upon those whom he eliminates are the unmistakable signs of lack of initiative, laziness, slowness of movement and speech, which also means slowness of thinking. Nine out of ten of them are men or women who just want jobs and have no realization that their job is their opportunity for self-expression. These are the clock watchers who do as little for their money as they have to instead of the rare few who do more than is expected of them for sheer love of work.

Every man who is on the lowest rungs of the ladder in any industry has as good a chance as any other one to become its president. Any good reader of character can look over all of those who are on those lower rungs and pick out one here and there out of hundreds. These are the ones who always get to the top, for they always make good at every stage of their advancement. That is the way the great industries find their strong men. Strength is written in them when they come, even as office boy, and the strength of character grows stronger year by year. One who has it always adds to it. He never subtracts from it.

In every industry, just as in every town, there are people who are very jealous of the success of others. These are the people of lesser ability than their co-workers or neighbors. These people develop strong cases of inferiority complexes and begin, in subtle ways, to underrate those who are superior to them. They cast little innuendoes which are intended to belittle those of whom they are jealous. What is known as the plant gossip, or the town gossip, is the fruit of such mediocre people. No more pitiable and despicable trait exists in Nature than inhuman gossip. Unlike the man who attacks you with a sword, from whom you have a chance to defend yourself, the gossip attacks her—or his—victims unseen. There is no way of protecting yourself from their viciousness. A good description of a gossip would be a human being with a serpent's tongue. That very appropriately describes one because their talking always stings. It is a strange fact that gossips gradually sculpture their features into serpentlike characteristics. Those who can read character in faces can always distinguish the inveterate, habitual gossip. Gossips always gossip to court favor for themselves. Their inferiority complex compels them to tear people down to a position inferior to themselves, or to an unmoral condition of contempt, in order to exalt themselves. It is not too complimentary to human nature that gossips find many ready listeners who drink gossip in eagerly and repeat it with much embroidery supplied by their imaginations. It is that eager pleasure which listeners to gossip exhibit which encourages them to return again and again with later news about their victims.

It may be comforting for your philosopher friend to assure you that no gossip can hurt you. That is true from the long-range point of view, but the immediate effect is very often cruelly hurtful. The story of the young girl who committed suicide because a gossip who saw her return home at 2 A.M. with a married man from the next town, spread so far and fast that she was practically ostracized by her entire neighborhood. Her death brought out the fact that she had been to a birthday dance party given by a friend in another town and her friend's father had driven her home.

From a purely philosophical point of view no gossiper or slanderer can hurt you in theory, for truth is stronger than untruth and comes uppermost in the long run. That may be comforting also from the long-range point of view, but gossipers can ruin one's business, break up homes, and destroy one's peace of mind over long intervals before the untruth of the gossipers can be known. In the meantime some victims can never recover.

All of this brings us back to the one great fact of life that love alone survives and love alone is loved. He who loves is loved. He who gives love, to him love is regiven. He who loves is the master sculptor who creates love in his own image. Any man who would succeed in the world can succeed in the measure in which the light of love can be seen written upon his countenance and glowing in his eyes. He who has sculptured love into his face cannot fail to be loved and honored by all men, no matter what his features are like or even though his body may be deformed.

The whole world loved and honored Charles Proteus Steinmetz, the world famous electrical genius and humanitarian to whom men of Edison's status paid deep homage. Steinmetz was a hunchback, but the sheer beauty of his character so deeply inspired anyone with whom he came into contact that his deformity was hardly noticed. He not only loved his work but loved people. Deeply etched in his features were not only the evidences of a meditative life, which characterizes the inner thinker, but also the love which characterizes those who love all people and all things.

The greatest and most beautiful character who ever lived is the One who most loved the world. It mattered not what His features were like, whether his hair was red or black, or whether he was tall or short. His would be the most beautiful face in all the world because love and beauty are one, and both were consummate in Him.

When you study the face of a man like Abraham Lincoln, or George Washington, you see great strength in their very beautiful faces but it is not the strength that makes them beautiful, it is the love for humanity and the consequent beauty of thought which does it. Lincoln's features were not at all well constructed. If Lincoln had not sculptured love upon that otherwise unattractive clay, it would be a very far stretch of the imagination to see beauty in it. You can see hundreds of his type without giving them a second glance. They are all of them Lincoln types in body only. Lincoln sculptured love into his clay and thus immortalized it with an enduring beauty which will awaken love in all who see his likeness forever.

Strength, without love, can never make a beautiful character, no matter how great he may become. I have in mind one of the strongest characters the world has ever known. He had the strength of a man whom you know would get anything he set out to get, or would accomplish anything he set out to accomplish. Such strength as that does not mean, however, that he is a beautiful character, it could indicate a sinister, or ominous, or selfish character whom you might fear to have dealings with, or would at least be on your guard against. When you meet that type of strong man you cannot possibly be drawn to him as you would be to a Benjamin Franklin.

The mere fact of having to live life with other people compels you to read the character of every life you come in contact with. Our very civilization compels this from us, for every person we come in contact with can affect our lives to the extent we permit him to affect it, and not beyond. If you, or I, are not a good judge of character, and permit people to enter our lives in any degree of association whatsoever, we are openly inviting that character to sculpture his thoughts upon our lives, our homes, our businesses or our friendships.

If you employ a houseworker, even though she has a kindly, honest face, but has in it a weakness which indicates inefficiency, or laziness, and your home is not as beautifully dusted as you would do it, your servant is writing her environment upon yours to your detriment. Likewise, if an industrialist employs managers and foremen who are hard-driving, selfish men to run his plant, even though they may have much knowledge and efficiency, the character of that plant is what they make it, even though the character of the employer is not like theirs. You may, therefore, sculpture efficiency, and strength, and similar qualities into the image you are making of yourself, and not become the kind of person whom a better judge of character would employ to manifest him.

You do not compliment a man by describing him as a strong man quite as much as you do when you describe him as a fine man. The connotation of love is in the description of a man as being fine, whereas the strong man description could as well apply to a Hitler as to a Lincoln.

To become a fine, strong character should be the supreme desire of every man who lives. First, however, comes the quality of love. All other qualities, such as efficiency, alertness, initiative and resourcefulness, which are built upon the basic quality of love, increase the measure of what he has sculptured into the image of himself. He may have all the other qualities, but without love sculptured in them he is poor indeed, and will remain so unto the end of his days. Look into your mirror and study the image you have created by your thinking. Is that the image you intended to create? Are you the kind of person you want to be? The reflection you see in that mirror is the individual you have created.

Out of fifty men in a department, why is it that one is selected to fill the vacancy of manager and not any of the others can even be considered? Why is it that out of over a hundred and fifty million people it is very difficult to find ten men whom the people of the country would feel happy and confident about becoming their President?

The answer is because the men who are chosen are the men whose thoughts and actions have expressed greater desire to manifest power and love than others who are not chosen.

Every man determines his own destiny by what he

thinks and does every moment of his life. You can become what you want to be only through your thoughts and actions, but the measure of your desire must be great in order for you to become great. Hitch your wagon to a star and fasten its bolts with deep desire to manifest love, and behold, its wings will carry you to those heights.

No one who has ever reached those heights has done so by himself alone. He who loves is aware of Love working with him. God is Love. Love is the foundation of the universe. He who deeply loves is deeply humble. The greatest men in the world are those who are most humble. An arrogant man is one who asserts his personal ego, while a humble man is one who suppresses it and is, therefore, without arrogance. The quality of humility is that which gives to one the gentleness and tenderness of a spiritual strength which can best be described as saintly.

This universe of love is a universe of law, for love is law. He who works with the law of love is working with the universe, and the universe is working with him.

Remember always that universal love is limitless, and you are the universe.

CHAPTER XVIII

You Create Your Own Destiny

Every man's destiny is of his own making. He is either its master or it masters him. He who has knowledge and desire may steer his ship of life anywhere he will, but he who has little knowledge and desire is not even aware that he has a rudder with which to steer his ship of life.

When you look out upon the sea of life you will find that there are very few really great men, very many mediocre men, and countless thousands of men whose measure of knowledge and desire is very low.

Why is this? Every man inherits all that God has to give. Nature does not deal unfairly or selectively with her gifts. The only difference between all men is a difference in *desire*—that one quality and nothing more. A man either desires to achieve or he does not desire to. He who deeply desires to achieve will gain the knowledge which he needs for achievement and the power to express that knowledge. Desire is always followed by willing effort. He who deeply desires anything loves the effort which he must exert to obtain his desire, but he whose desire is weak lacks incentive for effort and, therefore, makes none.

Every man who has ever become great becomes so only because he desired to, planned to, and made the effort to become so. There are no accidentally great men. *All great men build themselves in their own image. That which they become they first desired to become.* They thought out, and planned every step upward to their own high mountaintop. The great difference between all people lies not in their abilities but in the difference of intensity of desire to express their abilities.

It must be remembered that desire of Mind is the sole source of universal energy. The greater the intensity of desire in the Mind of any man, the greater power he has to express his ability. It follows as a matter of course that his achievement is greater.

Consider two men who desire to become great runners. Each has the same ability if both are normal at birth, but great desire gives a greater horsepower to ability than a lesser desire. The greater the desire the greater the measure of love that goes into every effort in daily training. Lesser desire lessens the measure of effort. Drudgery and monotony then creep into ability instead of love, and the work toward achievement ceases long before the man of intense desire even thinks of tiring. Desire to become a runner, and the effort of expressing that desire, builds the body in the image of a runner, but the excellence of the body itself is dependent solely upon the measure of desire to make the body excellent for its purpose. Two men of different measures of desire, therefore, create more or less excellent body machines which are appropriate to the purpose of running. The difference is in desire only, not in ability.

Demosthenes had less ability to become an orator than a man with a better speaking mechanism but his desire overcame that. It is well known that he increased his difficulty of speaking by putting pebbles in his mouth to improve his voice mechanism through difficult exercises. I knew a fine pianist who had less physical ability than another fine pianist for his fingers were short and stubby in comparison with the other's long, slim fingers, but desire was so strong in him that the handicap in physical disability disappeared.

To exemplify my meaning regarding the characteristic of Nature to build one's body in the image of one's desire, one need only to realize that the man who desires to be a runner becomes a runner with a runner's long, lithe supple body. He does not become a pugilist with a pugilist's stout, coarse muscular body. Had he commanded his body to become the body of a pugilist, instead of a runner, it would have obeyed his command as implicitly as it obeyed his command to become a runner. This exemplifies the fact that every man has command over matter to the extent that his desire to command it gives him the knowledge which enables him to command it.

Everyone knows that Theodore Roosevelt had a very weak body in childhood but the power of his intense desire to have a strong body gave him such command over the materials which constructed his body, that he became a very strong man physically. As a child he had very little endurance. He so forcefully commanded his body to become like the image he had in Mind that it became like it. Desire followed by effort will always command growing bodies.

My husband, who was an intimate friend of Theodore Roosevelt, as well as being official painter for his children, told me that before Mr. Roosevelt became President his greatest pleasure was in spending grueling hours on Western cattle ranches compelling his body to excel the work of every cowboy on the ranch. After he became President his great pleasures were chopping down trees in the early morning and taking long rides which called for great endurance. Very often, during those early days, he performed more than what the average man would call a good day's work before he actually began his regular day of work. Those who knew him well say that they never heard him say that he was tired.

One of the greatest demonstrations of the power of Mind to command matter is that of "Gill" Sonastine of Columbus, Ohio. This brave, spiritually illumined man has been completely paralyzed and blind for over thirty years during which time he has been unable to move a single muscle. His nerve system is so far beyond capability of repair that he cannot command it to recovery but he has commanded his body to survive so that he can manifest love to his fellow man through the only two functions left to him for creative expression, his hearing and his voice.

This amazing man is so vital and happy, mentally and spiritually, that by writing he earns an income sufficient for him to maintain a staff of attendants who take care of his physical and secretarial needs. He has hosts of friends and a great library of tape recordings of the memorable mental interchanges of their visits with him. I doubt if more than a few people who read his inspired writings know that he is utterly helpless physically, but so powerful mentally that he can command other bodies in his environment to give life to his creations by the power of his Mind alone. On one of my memorable visits to him he said to me: "I would rather have my body and what I know about God, than the perfect body of any man who does not know God as I do."

These examples illustrate the power which your Mind, or mine, has to command our bodies to multiply our ability to fulfill the physical demands of our destiny.

We also have equal power of Mind to control the spiritual unfoldings of our destinies. No matter what you
may desire to become in life, or whatever spiritual height
you desire to ascend, you can attain that height if your
desire is strong enough to be followed by the necessary
actions which will elevate you to that height. No heights
can ever be attained by wishful thinking or desire not followed by action. Whatever work you perform with deep
desire, God will work with you by doing exactly as much
for you as you do to manifest Him. The farmers, or
gardeners, or foresters know this. They know that a little
work given by them brings but little work done by Nature. The giving and regiving are always equal. The
more service you give to Nature the more Nature will
work with you in her regivings.

*Whatever destiny you plan for yourself that destiny
you can reach if your desire to reach it is strong enough.
Desire alone is the controlling factor, not money, nor
family, nor position. No one's influence can make you
great. You alone control your own destiny.*

How many people utterly fail because of blaming other
conditions and circumstances for their failures. A certain
inventor, who had a wonderful idea, solicited capital
from his friends for years to carry out his idea, then laid
the blame for his failure upon his inability to raise capital. He wasted so much time trying to secure large capital
instead of small capital to take one step at a time, that he
failed utterly.

Thomas Edison, on the contrary, took one little step at
a time to unfold the growth of his idea. His idea was a very
big one, a very revolutionary one, yet he did not try to
raise millions to finance it. He needed only a few dollars
to take his first step. Every step after that took care of it-

self as it appeared. He always had enough money to make one step at a time. Had he started by raising the millions which finally revolutionized the lighting industry, he would probably have failed as the inventor above-quoted failed. His desire, persistence and resourcefulness were worth more to him in unfolding his destiny than all the money in the world.

How many thus give alibis for their failures: "I cannot do it because I do not know anyone in Washington who will give me letters of introduction to the higher ups," one will say. Another will say: "I was unable to go to college," and blame his failure on that. Over and over again you will hear people say: "He was lucky. Everyone gave him a break." One such man said to the father of a famous motion-picture star: "How lucky your son is." "Yes, he is lucky," the father replied, "and the funny thing about it is that the harder he works the luckier he is."

Charles Goodyear transformed world transportation from the five miles an hour buggy days to the seventy miles an hour vulcanized rubber age. No one can ever attribute his success to luck. Every upward step of his progress was agonizing. One misfortune after another confronted him which seemed to be the end of his road. Once during his upward climb, he was heralded as a great world benefactor. It was thought that he had succeeded in vulcanizing rubber and fortunes were invested in making rubber overshoes for winter snows, and in filling a huge government contract for rubber mailbags. These were highly successful during cold weather but when warm weather came they partially melted into a sticky condition which rendered them utterly useless for their purpose, except in winter.

Perhaps no greater blow ever befell an inventor. It would have killed many other weaker men than Goodyear. Even though all financial support became impossible he continued, although his closest friends deserted him. He became so poor that he had no money to bury his dead child. It is said that his wife and he had to bury it in the woods of Woburn, as no one in the town would advance further money and he would not accept charity.

Later on his wife was very ill at a time when he was making his last possible experiment with the last of his natural rubber supplies. He had broken his furniture to keep the fire going for his experiment, and to keep the room warm which was occupied by his sick wife. She suddenly called out to him in distress. Leaving his boiling pot he rushed to her room, forgetting all about his kettle while attending to her wants. Then came what seemed to be the final tragedy. The pot boiled over and all of his last precious rubber went into the fire. Seizing a fork, but with little hope of saving it, he immediately recognized the unmistakable signs which he had been looking for all those years. That accident demonstrated that wet heat and boiling would not vulcanize. It needed the dry heat of fire.

Perhaps there is no greater demonstration of the control of one's destiny by man himself than the life story of Charles Goodyear. Likewise, there is no better demonstration of the adulation one's friends and neighbors bestow upon neighbors after they are dead, whom they have ignored while alive, than the story of the people of Woburn who gathered together about fifteen years ago to erect a tablet to his memory in the town and express their pride in their honored neighbor.

How ludicrous it would be to say that Goodyear was

lucky, or that Wagner, Brahms, the Wright brothers or Marconi were lucky. There is no finer example in American history than that of the belief of the Wright brothers that their destiny in life was to conquer air as a means of transportation for men. An age-old adage says: "You can no more do what you are trying to do than you can fly." The Wright brothers not only disproved this assumption but did it under the most difficult circumstances. I believe it would be easier to secure capital today to build spaceships for interplanetary transportation, than it was in their day to raise any money for so foolhardy an idea as to build ships for man to fly in the air.

As they could raise no money they earned the money in a little bicycle repair shop. With the greatest economy and patience, coupled with hard work and an endurance born out of belief in their power to control their own destiny, the Wright brothers actually flew. Then one of the most thwarting things in human history happened. So strong was the belief that man could not fly that the official world denied that they flew for a long time after they had actually flown.

When it was finally admitted that human beings could fly, millions of dollars could be raised more easily than tens could be raised before the fact was demonstrated. This fact is not of prime import in this story. What is of import is the fact that anyone who strongly believes in a heaven-born inspiration given to him as knowledge of his destiny, can fulfill that destiny. In doing so, however, he must know that creation means the expression of energy in work. One must not only be willing to work but love to work. Willingness is not enough. Willingness has some reservations in its connotation. The creative Mind must have no reservation. Whatever hurdles he must confront he must meet with joy and full knowledge that he can surmount them, and love the challenge of surmounting them.

Those who do nothing because they cannot raise money to help them should realize that a very large percentage of the world's greatest men were born into poor families and had to work against terrific odds to get their first small start. They not only did not have money, they also did not have schooling. Many of them were also country boys who were raised in sparsely peopled back country, and did not have even the possibilities for opportunity which cities held.

Abraham Lincoln was one of these. When you see a barefoot country boy driving his cattle home from pasture, it is a far stretch of the imagination to think of that boy becoming able to transform world practice, as Lincoln did. It is not safe to assume that he will not do so, however, for inklings of his destiny may have already whispered to his inner Consciousness. So many country boys in this country, and peasant boys in Europe, have become world geniuses, inventors or statesmen that it is safe to bow deeply before one out of the many with a feeling of certainty that he will make history some day.

Every great man or woman who has ever lived was once an obscure child whom no one would pick out as a world figure. In the heart of one of the many of them was a clear picture of his destiny as he could see himself in the mirror. From that moment on he reached out for his destiny by taking one step at a time until he reached its highest step. During that journey he always met with tremendous difficulties, but every man who knows his destiny knows also that he will reach it.

The only way that you can command your own destiny

is to first vision it mentally. Make as clear a picture of it in your Mind as you can, then take one little step at a time in unfolding it. Each step will give you a clearer picture of that destiny ahead and will bring you one step nearer to it. Never say, "I cannot do it because I do not know how to do it." *Start doing it and learn how to do it in the doing of it.*

Anyone knows how to take one step in the direction of his desire. When he takes that step he can more clearly see his next step. Edison's little three dollar battery was a first step toward his goal. He knew how to take that step, but he had to take it before he could know what the next step would be for him.

You and I, and everyone on earth, are in that same position. We all had to start the same way. How many finish the race with honors is dependent only upon themselves. And those who do win the race of life with honors win it only because they either intuitively feel, or dynamically know, that God is working with them as they work in harmony with Him.

CHAPTER XIX

Conclusion and God's Message to Women

The whole journey of life is for the sole purpose of knowing God. Every moment of it, from your very beginning, God is working with you to inspire you with His ever Presence, which centers you in your Soul.

Man has heard God's Silent Voice within him for millions of years, but he did not know what it was. He called it instinct. He did not even know that instinct was not only God's Voice within his Soul, but it was also an electric beam which guided and controlled the unfolding of all God's creations.

Consciousness dawned in man and he began to think with God's Mind. God's Mind talks to man through his Soul, but in his early beginnings he did not know that he thought with God's Mind. For millions of years he had but sensed with his body. He sought sensations for his body. He sought survival for his body. Then, later, he sought possessions for his body. His entire sense of existence was through his body. He even sought happiness through his body, not knowing that the Soul alone could know happiness and that it could never be found through sensations of the body alone.

Genius dawned in man. He then knew the Mind of man and Mind of God were One. When God then talked to man, he knew that God talked to him, and he then talked with God. When God talked to early man through instinct, He but commanded him. When God and cosmic genius-man talked together through inspiration, God then communed with him. When man thus knew God and communed with Him, God sent messages through him to other men, who did not know Him.

That has been God's way since man's beginning. Through those who know God, He sends inspired messages to those who do not know Him, to inspire them to know Him. He first sends messages of His love in the rhythms of His love. Through His cosmic geniuses, who know Him, He slowly attunes the heartbeat of man's thinking to His mighty rhythms to draw men closer unto Him. Beauty comes into the world through the heart of man thus inspired with those mighty rhythms of God's universal thinking. The poets give God's messages to man. The builders of temples, and the inspired man of God who chisels the symmetry and balance of beauty into white marble, these also give God's messages to man to bring him ever closer to knowing God within his own Soul.

The prophets who knew God told men of His love. God spoke to messengers, like Buddha, Zoroaster and Mohammed, who knew His Voice, and the meaning of it. He gave messages to them for His people. God gave the same messages to all their peoples, but they did not know that God spoke to them. God speaks to all creatures of His Creation, but they do not know that He speaks to them.

Birds do not know how to build nests, or to fly south, or why. God shows them how and directs their flight by polarity control. Spiders do not know how to build webs, nor to calculate their necessary stresses and strains. God works with them and tells them how. His Presence centers the spider and ant to manifest His love with the same care that He gives to man. That is what is meant by God's Omnipresence.

God is everywhere, for Mind is everywhere. Every particle of creating matter, and every forming body, are centered by the Soul-Mind, from within, to control it, and two so-called magnetic poles are extended from that center to guide, and balance it. Just as the center of gravity and the two poles of this earth balance and control its every movement and relationship to other planets, so is man centered and controlled. Man can defy that control if he desires to do so, but his defiance is costly to him in many ways. In animals and the elements of matter, which living bodies are created from, there is no defiance of that law, hence Nature is always in balance.

We have heard much about revelations having been given to prophets and saints of olden days. God's revelations are just as much a part of today's communion between man and God, as they ever were. God reveals Himself to you, and to all of us, every moment of our lives. You suddenly know something which you did not know one minute before. It comes to you in a timeless flash. That is God telling you what you have desired to know. That desire to know is a wordless prayer which you do not even know that you have uttered, but God knows of your desire and extends the answer to you through His thinking. That is what revelations are. You are constantly being enriched by revelations from God. You may not know it yet. That is the slow process of your unfolding from your dark to His Light. Aeons pass before men become aware of it. There are those, however, who have become aware of it and they give their knowing of God's messages to man.

When God "revealed Himself" to Moses, and told him to lead his people out of Egypt, He also revealed Himself to all of Moses' people. They did not know it, however, but Moses did, for Moses knew God's Silent Voice and fully comprehended its meaning. He, therefore, told those who did not know God's Voice what God had commanded them to do. That is what is meant by being a messenger to man from God.

There have been many messengers who have brought beauty and love to their fellowmen but as yet all too few have become aware of the mighty rhythms and whisperings of God's Silent Voice speaking to them from His kingdom of heaven within their Soul.

If you do not talk to God as you work with Him it is because you do not *know* that you can. *That is the only reason.* You can talk to God this moment if you will but believe you can and deeply desire to. He talks to you through your Soul as He works with you to gradually awaken you to the Light of His glorious Presence. Why not desire to know God now as He works with you, and you work with Him, to unfold your destiny? Some day you will become aware of that wonderful fact that you can talk to God as He has forever talked with you while He has been working with you. You will then work more intelligently with Him when you *know* that you are working with Him, instead of not knowing it. That day must someday come to you. Why not begin now, knowing that He is awaiting that day when you will know the joy and ecstasy of His Presence within you. That is what the words in The Divine Iliad Message mean, which say:

"All men will come to Me in due time, but theirs is the agony of awaiting."

Such men as Beethoven, Mozart, Brahms, Leonardo or Whitman knew that they could talk to God as He worked with them, and they brought rhythmic messages of Beauty from God to man in a language which all men can comprehend within their very Soul. The whole world of men can talk to God directly, if they but know that they can. They do not need Brahms or Beethoven to act as interpreter for them when they know that all of God's Omniscient thinking is theirs when they will but "tune in with it," as Brahms and Beethoven did. Omniscience is universal. Each man can know all things when he desires to know all things.

Deep within my Consciousness I have known my destiny since childhood. I cannot remember a time that I did not talk to God for He was the first one I told my thoughts to and later took my human problems to. God has always been more real to me than any human being could possibly be. Seeing such unhappiness in the world gave birth within me to a deep desire to share the knowledge of God's great love and direction with others. And so it was that God commanded me to give this message to you.

Likewise, as all women desire to give love, I know there have been many down through the ages who have faintly heard God's whispering command to them to take their place as the World-Mother. This book is God's Message to you. God has told you what you should do to save this civilization and cause it to endure. I can but do as I am commanded, for which every moment of my life is dedicated. I cannot execute the command alone. The mothers of the world can bring order out of chaos, unity out of disunity, and LOVE out of FEAR, if they will but take the empty seat beside the Father of the world-home to give it a Mother's Love.

I will close this message, as I opened it, to tell you that *the eleventh hour is here.* You cannot wait, lest the world perish. You must unite now by multiplying the power of your voice by millions before the next election. Chapter XII has outlined the plan. Further details will follow at the end of this chapter.

I will say to you, however, that when God plainly tells His children what to do to work with Him to unfold His children's destiny, He will work with them to unfold it.

Mankind desires Peace—and Love—and Romance— and Beauty. And all peoples of the whole world desire joy in their hearts and the singing of Hosannas in their homes. The world can have its desire fulfilled *when it works with God,* but not while it works against Him. God made fathers and mothers in equally divided pairs in order that they could unite as equal pairs. God intended that male aggressive and progressive qualities, which construct the world-home, should be balanced by the female qualities which give cohesiveness of love to the world-home. Man has forever been taking life. Woman has forever been giving life. *The world-family-home can endure only by balancing the male-female qualities.*

God's Silent Voice has forever been telling the fathers and mothers of the world that Peace, Happiness, Romance and Beauty can come only through their unity. There has never been unity between the fathers and mothers of the world. However, the world's desire for happiness can never be fulfilled until balance between the two equally divided mate-pairs makes the desired unity possible.

If the Mothers of the world will but obey God's Voice, and if the Fathers of the world will but open their hearts to the balance of Unity in World-Father-Motherhood, "the peace which passeth all understanding" WILL COME TO PASS.

The Walter Russell Foundation

SWANNANOA, WAYNESBORO, VIRGINIA

ITS PLAN AND PURPOSE

The Walter Russell Foundation was formed for the purpose of giving to the world-family The Message of the Divine Iliad, by Walter Russell, which is a scientific explanation of God's ways and processes in the construction of His universe, and the Message of a Living Philosophy, by Lao Russell, for illumining man's Cosmic way of Life in his long journey of life from the dark to God's Light.

These two purposes are ONE, for one gives man the knowledge of how to live life and manifest His Creator, and the other gives him knowledge of what Life is and his relation to his Creator.

We fully realize that the human race is in its very early stages and can advance only as new knowledge comes into the world to make one know what life is for, and why God put man here to live it. We fully realize that our present-day world disunity is entirely due to our primacy, and the attendant ignorance of the basic essentials of knowing how to live life. We are still in the stage where our greatest values are money and transient physical possessions, instead of the enduring spiritual values of mutual service of man to man.

This early stage of man's unfolding is the cause of wars which men institute to acquire the physical possessions of others for themselves. That stage of greed for power over others, and the physical possessions of others, must be entirely eliminated from human consciousness before a

Swannanoa—Headquarters of the Walter Russell Foundation
Sculpture Gardens of the Works of Walter and Lao Russell

happy race of humanity is possible. To exalt mankind above this present low physical level to the higher spiritual level, which all men will eventually reach, The Walter Russell Foundation has instituted a course of study which gives the knowledge required by man to tell him of himself, his purpose on earth, the laws which govern his own Being, and those concerning his relationship to other men and to Nature.

The main foundation of these studies is a one-year Home Study Course, issued monthly in four-lesson units, entitled UNIVERSAL LAW, NATURAL SCIENCE AND LIVING PHILOSOPHY. This course of study was written by both Walter and Lao Russell. It has already reached the far corners of the world, even to such remote places as New Zealand, South Africa, South America, Hawaii, Finland, Greece, Iran and of course England and Scotland.

Wherever it is reaching, its students are becoming transformed by the knowledge given them of Nature which they have never before been able to obtain. Man must first know about man, himself. That is the first essential of life. A way of life through a living philosophy based upon a knowledge of the laws of Nature, which govern man, is of the greatest import.

As students have become transformed through the new knowledge they have gained, others have become inspired to do likewise, and that is the way this course of study has spread around the world. The demand is now growing so fast in other non-English-speaking countries for this new knowledge, that we are now preparing to translate our Home Study Course and books into all other languages.

Ill health and the misfortunes of life are the result of not knowing how to obey Natural law. When man learns how to obey Natural law he can then command his life.

We teach the power of Mind to command one's own body and keep its normal balance of health. This enables people to heal themselves through Cosmic knowledge. We are not consultants in health matters, nor do we practice Mind healing in any way or manner. It is interesting to know, however, how many of our students are healing themselves of various illnesses because of this basic new knowledge of Nature's ways and processes.

This Foundation was chartered as a non-profit educational institution in 1948 under the laws of Virginia, by Lao Russell for two purposes: 1, to see her famous husband's works of art gathered together as a Shrine of Beauty to perpetuate for posterity and, 2, to unite mankind into one world-family upon the basis of brotherly love in human interchange, instead of brotherly conquest of man by man, which has been the basis of world human relations for thousands of years.

The more immediate purpose of the Foundation is to save our rapidly decaying civilization from another fall into chaos by bringing the balance of unity between the World-Father and the World-Mother, in order that the management of the World-Family will have the qualities of both the Father and the Mother in its WORLD-HOME.

Those who desire to know more about the books and teachings of Lao and Dr. Walter Russell should write to The University of Science and Philosophy, Swannanoa, Waynesboro, Virginia 22980